Managing Healthy Organizations

DATE

28.00

Routledge Studies in Human Resource Development

EDITED BY MONICA LEE, LANCASTER UNIVERSITY, UK

HRD theory is changing rapidly. Recent advances in theory and practice, how we conceive of organisations and of the world of knowledge, have led to the need to reinterpret the field. This series aims to reflect and foster the development of HRD as an emergent discipline.

Encompassing a range of different international, organisational, methodological and theoretical perspectives, the series promotes theoretical controversy and reflective practice.

Managing Healthy Organizations

Worksite Health Promotion and the New
Self-Management Paradigm

**Mikael Holmqvist and
Christian Maravelias**

Routledge
Taylor & Francis Group

NEW YORK AND LONDON

First published 2011
by Routledge
711 Third Avenue, New York, NY 10017

Simultaneously published in the UK
by Routledge
2 Park Square, Milton Park, Abingdon, Oxon OX14 4RN

Routledge is an imprint of the Taylor & Francis Group, an informa business

First published in paperback 2012

Typeset in Sabon by Taylor & Francis

Library of Congress Cataloging-in-Publication Data
Holmqvist, Mikael, 1970–
Managing healthy organizations : worksite health promotion and the new self-management paradigm / Mikael Holmqvist and Christian Maravelias.
p. cm. – (Routledge studies in human resource development; v. 18)
Includes bibliographical references and index.
1. Employee health promotion. 2. Industrial hygiene. I. Maravelias, Christian, 1967– II. Title.
RC969.H43H65 2010
658.3'82–dc22
2010006686

ISBN 13: 978-0-415-87389-5 (hbk)
ISBN 13: 978-0-203-84580-6 (ebk)
ISBN 13: 978-0-415-65553-8 (pbk)

Contents

Preface

This book studies worksite health promotion as a way of managing organizations. It examines the character of corporate health experts' work, the social contexts of their profession, their striving for influence, the way they try to affect people's thinking and behavior, and especially the organizational ethic and culture that they contribute to construct. The book does not primarily treat these issues abstractly. Rather, it reports first-hand fieldwork from the health-promoting activities as exercised by company doctors, nurses, ergonomics, behavioral experts and other professionals in Scania, a renowned international corporation in the automotive industry. Corporate health experts are typically not regarded as 'managers' in the organization studies literature. However, our observations suggest that even though their activities are grounded in a medical enterprise and concern the observation and treatment of individual people from a clinical point of view, their work is closely aligned with problems relating to the general management of organizations. Through a focused appraisal of this institutionally central albeit neglected occupational group in management studies, this book tries to explore and understand in some depth situations and experiences that are of general interest and concern in our society.

We owe a great deal to many people. First, we would like to thank all the people that we met at Scania, and particularly the employees of Scania's Health and Work Environment Unit. They have all patiently educated us in how their world works. We owe a large thanks to its manager, Stefan Persson. We regard his support as an expression of his genuine interest in academic research, as well as his courage and curiosity in allowing us to explore the activities of the organization that he is in charge of. His deputies Carina Albiin-Svensk, Gunnar Hedlund and Anders Tholerud have also been most helpful and supportive, and have always taken time to answer our questions and straighten out our queries. Riitta Holappa has been very helpful in organizing the many meetings and observations that we have conducted. We also wish to thank Eric Giertz, a specialist on Scania, for proposing a number of valuable suggestions on how to interpret our observations. Our second debt goes to the persons at AstraZeneca, TeliaSonera, Statistics Sweden, Lantmännen, Previa, Adecco and Systembolaget whom we met in the early phase of this research. They were all very kind to inform us on their respective worksite health promotion activities that gave us useful preliminary feedback on our emerging research questions. Particular thanks go to Camilla Clereus at AstraZeneca who organized a number of interviews with her colleagues and also provided us with relevant documents on AstraZeneca's commitment in trying to create a 'healthy organization.'

This study is part of our research program *Managing Healthy Organizations* that is funded by the Jan Wallander and Tom Hedelius Research Foundation for Social Science. This book is an expression of our commitment to study work, health and welfare from an organization sociologist's point of view. Earlier, we have suggested that health can be seen as an interesting topic for students of organizations and a number of our colleagues were kind to propose different avenues of research within such a program (see Holmqvist and Maravelias, 2006). We have also outlined how worksite health promotion can be regarded as an expression of corporate social responsibility with concomitant implications for social control (Holmqvist, 2009), as well as an 'extended' and 'obscure' form of power in so-called post-bureaucratic organizations (Maravelias, 2009). Our research program seeks to extend a common and familiar view of management in contemporary research that revolves around the notion of 'self-management' by exploring organizational initiatives in the name of health that we believe has interesting potential for theory development as well as debate and reflection in society at large.

The research would not have been possible without strong support from our employer the School of Business of Stockholm University that has enabled us to spend time for both fieldwork and writing. For many insightful comments and critique we are indebted to our friends and colleagues Johan Hansson, Hans Hasselbladh, Konstantin Lampou, Per Skålén and Alexander Styhre. We also want to thank our students who have listened patiently and responded creatively to our grapplings with the data. Thanks are also due to the participants at a seminar held at the School of Business in December, 2009, where we presented our main ideas and findings.

Finally, we thank our amazing wives Maria and Camilla, and our wonderful sons Gabriel and Samuel, and Arthur and Axel. With love we dedicate this work to them.

Mikael Holmqvist
Christian Maravelias
Stockholm, January 2010

1 Introduction

In the aftermath of major transformations in the economic and political systems, which relate to notions of globalization and post-industrialization, increasingly, scholarly and popular attention has moved to 'flexible,' 'innovation-driven,' 'explorative' and 'entrepreneurial' organizations. Such organizations are straining traditional management practices and systems of control. Rather than strict technical and bureaucratic regulations, these organizations are said to require a new management paradigm that empowers individuals and encourages responsibility and initiative.

On the basis of such observations, the popular management literature has filled a large quantity of books and journal articles with a multitude of models and ideas that all convey the promise of helping organizations replace traditional modes of control that are based on a technical and formally hierarchical regulation of the work processes with new, subtler forms of managerial influence and authority that seek to win employees' commitment, dedication, enthusiasm and involvement. Scholarly contributions to this discourse have pointed out that these new types of control operate through shared cultural values and norms (e.g. Halal, 1994; Heckscher, 1994; Hogget, 1991; Volberda, 1998). The notion of 'corporate culture' is treated both as an important managerial philosophy and as a technology for instilling devotion to work and to the organization's mission. Properly managed corporate culture is seen to build a sense of direction into highly informal, 'post-bureaucratic procedures' (Kunda, 1992; Savage, 1996). Hence, the main task of corporate managers in contemporary organizations is no longer the direct control of employees, but the institutionalization of shared basic values on the basis of which empowered and self-governed work become possible (e.g. Drucker, 1988; Heckscher and Donnellon, 1994; Kanter, 1990; Mintzberg, 1998).

The existing critique of this discourse has primarily addressed issues of organizational power and individual autonomy and identity. It is commonly argued that the new cultural controls operate not merely 'on the surface' of employees, forcing or motivating them to behave in ways which are aligned with corporate visions and goals; they also 'seep' into the very identities of individuals, constituting them as particular types of subjects who manage themselves in accordance with corporate values (e.g. Alvesson and Willmott, 2002; Casey, 1999; Covaleski *et al.*, 1998; Deetz, 1998; DuGay, 2000). Hence, the new cultural controls are regarded as mechanisms of power that make individuals' freedom of choice not an element to be restricted, but a key resource in the workings of power (Maravelias, 2003). Whereas managerially endorsed cultural programs can be understood as explicit expressions of the ideological function of corporate culture, 'human resource management' (HRM) is regarded as the specific representation of certain technologies whose main task it is to substantiate the corporate culture (Casey, 1999; Townley, 1994). In essence, HRM techniques make up 'appropriate individuals' who can be trusted with considerable autonomy because they subscribe to the culture of the organization (Alvesson and Willmott, 2002; Covaleski *et al.*, 1998; Townley, 1994). According to this view, HRM techniques such as assessment centers, performance appraisals, attitude surveys, mentoring, etc. discipline employees by accumulating knowledge about them, which can then be used to advise and persuade them to work on themselves in order to even further align them to corporate norms and values. In that HRM techniques are based on knowledge about employees, they exercise a kind of power in organizations that are at once more intimate and intense, and at the same time more invisible and unobtrusive; HRM appears less as an exercise of power and more as a form of care for employees (see Barratt, 2002: 2003; Townley, 1994).

It is in this familiar context that the recent phenomenon of worksite health promotion (WHP) can be explored and conceptualized. Certainly, as stressed by Conrad and Walsh (1992), within the field of organization studies there has been a long interest in the reciprocal relationship between work and health. The majority of studies bear a direct relation to the gradual growth, from the 1920s and onwards, of industrial health programs in large corporations, which institutionalized a corporate medical presence in the workplace and established occupational medicine as a recognized speciality. However, just like these programs, the studies of work and health have addressed problems directly associated with work. A distinction has typically been made between health on and off the job, and a line has been drawn between work and private life. Hence, relatively little interest has been given to how contemporary WHP programs in fact challenge the traditional distinction between work and private life. Furthermore, most studies of work and health have tended to take for granted that health programs are primarily aligned with employees' interests and that they are instigated by various reform movements and workers' struggles to expose and reduce hazards related to their work. This has resulted in little attention being given to the other side of the work–health nexus: How employers factor health considerations into workforce management and productivity control. Typical WHP programs such as lifestyle examinations and coaching, accident prevention, risk behavior assessment, help to self-help, etc. indicate that measures which are taken for employees' health are becoming parts of a new, more encompassing form of managerial control of employees. As expressed by Conrad and Walsh (ibid.), the advancement of modern WHP programs may be a sign of a new corporate health ethic that seeks to manage the 'whole employee' and especially what the employees may become, the risks they face and the abilities they have to shoulder for developing their selves into a real corporate value.

From the 1990s onward, corporate management has come to take an active role in promoting the health of employees (e.g. MacIntosh *et al.*, 2007; Zoller, 2003). For instance, in the special issue "Managerial Dimensions of Organizational Health: The Healthy Leader at Work" of the *Journal of Management Studies*, Quick *et al.* (2007) stressed that "for organizations to maintain their vitality, their productivity, and their competitive edge requires executives and leaders who are healthy, strong, and capable." Management gurus like Stewart Friedman argue that "people that feel better in all domains of their lives ... perform better" (2008a: 112). Such ambitions resound well with the basic tenets of health promotion that is defined as "the process of enabling people to increase control over, and to improve, their health" (WHO, 2010). The definition indicates that health promotion is rooted in a critique of traditional occupational medicine's restricted focus on individuals' bio-psychological problems and, in that connection, its treatment of individuals as passive objects. It is commonly argued that long-term health and well-being presupposes, on the one hand, that individuals actively take part in managing their health and, on the other hand, that a holistic focus on family relations, working life, and—in particular—lifestyles is used when examining and promoting individuals' health (Downie *et al.*, 1996; Hanson, 2007). Hence, whether or not an individual can be defined as 'healthy' is from this perspective not merely a question of bodily and psychological issues; it is also a question of his or her motivation to work on maintaining and improving desired social abilities and competencies.

This view of health—as comprising individuals' lifestyles and their commitment to become 'better'—is interesting from the perspective of contemporary work organizations as it stresses an integration of work and private life. In organizations that pursue WHP programs, the ambitions of improving employees' health and well-being are not limited to the circumstances underlying and circumscribing the work their employees do; they also concern employees' activities away from work (see Zoller, 2003). WHP programs typically underline the importance of maintaining a balance between the professional and the private lives of employees (MacDonald, 1998). Ultimately, this is not about protecting employees' health and well-being from the intrusion of work into the sphere of private life. Rather, it is to organize work and private life into a productive balance. According to the discourse on WHP, the professional and the private spheres of life are not assumed to be at odds with each other. On the contrary, 'healthy individuals' are typically seen as being able to work harder and longer, especially if their work is stimulating—and stimulating work is by itself regarded as positive for individuals' health (Ziglio *et al.*, 1999; Gillies, 1998).

More specifically, four principles appear to be central to such synergies: First, employees' situation at work should be approached holistically (Davies and Macdonald, 1998). Management should consider how its decisions affect employees' lives and whether or not employees' lifestyles make them up to the challenges that management lets them face. Second, management should further the development of an honest and 'family-like' atmosphere where interaction and cooperation between colleagues is genuine as opposed to formal (Hanson, 2007; Wilkinson, 1999). Third, individuals should be empowered with enough autonomy to handle their tasks flexibly and with self-control (Docherty *et al.*, 2002; Kira 2000). Finally, management must respect and secure employees' need of maintaining a balance between professional life and private life (O'Donnell, 2002). Largely consistent with the dominant management paradigm of corporate cultures, active and self-regulating employees, work *should* be infused with personal values and genuine motivation and commitment; colleagues *should* be friends; and cooperation *should* be informal rather than formal. Together, this makes work a very direct and integrated part of life in general.

Through a qualitative case study of the health-promoting activities as exercised by corporate health experts at the internationally leading manufacturer of heavy trucks, buses and coaches Scania (www.scania.com), this book explores how WHP operates as a specific form of management of employees, expanding the principles of control of corporate culture programs and traditional human resource management techniques. In the Appendix, a detailed account of the research process is proposed. In short, over the course of one year we interviewed 118 persons (including representatives from other companies than Scania); conducted a number of sessions of participant observations; and collected documents and other archival material that were of relevance to the study. The efficiency of Scania's WHP comes from its potential to establish forms of management and control, which do not appear as or are not presented as management. More specifically, its WHP opens up a subtle and unobtrusive form of exercising power, first, because it comes forth as a form of expert-based care for the employees, and, second, because it does not operate through authoritative directives and instructions, but through the informed and free choices of the employees themselves. In this sense it addresses employees' potential to manage all aspects of their lives in a committed, energetic and enthusiastic way. The basic observation of our study is that WHP programs are based on an internalization of self-discipline and self-control; WHP instils in employees the proper motivation and the proper knowledge for people to control themselves along the lines of a 'healthy life' and a 'good career.' In this respect, WHP programs involve much more than reducing health costs and furthering the subjective well-being of single employees; they are primarily about controlling productivity by shaping values and attitudes of employees toward lifestyles which are aligned with corporate cultures that reward activity, motivation, self-discipline and responsibility.

The book is outlined in the following way: In chapter 2 we discuss literature on organizational control. In particular we outline the major transformations in organizational control regimes that have taken place during the twentieth century and address how these organizational control regimes are seen by organizational scholars to relate to employees' health and well-being. The chapter suggests how organizational control has generally been taken to be at odds with employees' health and well-being. However, the review also stresses that with the advent of contemporary 'concertive' forms of control in organizations, organizational control, and employees' health and well-being are increasingly seen as mutually supportive. The concertive control regime breaks with previous control regimes' sharp distinction between the professional and private self that is seen to underlie its potential of at once generating a more encompassing control of employees' behavior and of furthering employees' health and well-being.

These points are important for the ideas we put forth in chapter 3, where we explore literature on health promotion and particularly workplace health promotion. The chapter suggests how contemporary health promotion programs and activities have developed from a critique of the restricted focus of traditional medicine on individual illness and disease, and its lack of attention to the whole life situation of the individual. Furthermore, it stresses how the tendency of health promotion programs and activities to establish non-hierarchical relations between the health expert and the individual around broad lifestyle issues opens up a link to contemporary concertive control regimes. In this sense health promotion and concertive control alike are based on the idea that individuals become healthier and more efficient if they become self-managing and, in that connection, if they are given opportunities to bring together the professional and private spheres of their lives. It is, we suggest, here that health promotion conveys a potential of becoming a significant part of the concertive control regimes of contemporary organizations. For whereas the concertive control regime requires individuals that are able to autonomously govern their work and private lives into a fruitful and healthy balance, health promotion is specifically focused on making up this self-managing and active individual.

In order to substantiate the theoretical ideas as outlined in chapters 1–3, we then go on to explore the interrelations between the worksite health promotion activities of Scania and its production and management system. In chapter 4 we account for the principles of a new production and management system that was established by Scania in the early to mid 1990s. Whereas the old production and management system operated according to traditional 'technical' and 'bureaucratic' control principles, leading to problems related to employee health and well-being; the new production and management system has emphasized employees' commitment, activity and autonomy in structuring their own work, and has, according to Scania, resulted in a substantially reduced absence due to sickness and poor health among the employees. The ideal employee in the new production and management system is not the traditional, obedient factory worker who willingly does what he or she is told; but an active, social and reflective individual who is able to manage his or her own work and continuously seeks to improve his or her abilities. In chapter 5 we turn toward the Health and Work Environment unit at Scania and account for how it began to develop and grow at about the same time as Scania sought to establish its new production and management system. By emphasizing that employees should remain healthy in the sense of being committed, active and motivated both on and off the job, Scania's health organization can be seen as a close ally to the new system's ambition to create a new attitude and mindset among the employees which centers on their ability to manage themselves. We account for this organization's main policies and its overall organizational structure and functioning, particularly emphasizing the interplay between the health professionals (such as company doctors, ergonomic experts and behavioral experts) and the management team in pursuing health-promoting activities for all of Scania's employees. In chapter 6 we address how the health organization through its programs and activities both adapts to the demands and requirements of the new production regime, and how it actively tries to shape the basic principles of that regime. Specific attention is given to how the health professionals negotiate with managers in the production line and how they try to contribute to supporting employees to make them able to cope with the new requirements of 'constant improvements' that is at the core of the production system. In chapter 7 we turn toward the specific programs and services (e.g. health counselling and screening, and physical exercise programs) that the health organization and its different professionals provide, and we seek to show the social and individual effects that they attempt to bring about among the employees and Scania's organization.

In chapter 8 we conclude the study by outlining how the health promotion activities and programs that we have studied at Scania operate as a specific form of managing Scania's employees. In all, our study of Scania suggests that concerns for the health of employees and corporate economics do not lead in two different directions, but may in fact be joined so that measures taken for the health of the employees become directly linked to the measures taken for the economic well-being of the corporation; not only or even primarily in the sense of reducing costs for absence due to sickness, but rather in the sense of creating more committed, able and motivated employees who are willing to work hard in order to execute the principles of modern management. Our study furthermore suggests that the link between employees' health and corporate economic concerns are provided through a new form of managing employees, which is defined by a caring and therapeutic ethos. We conclude that although this new management regime has considerable potential to make way for at once more efficient forms of work, it also conveys risks of making ill-health and incapacities to perform one's work a result of employees' moral inadequacies.

In chapter 9, finally, we discuss the broader social and political implications of the health-oriented management regime that we have studied. This discussion centers on the notion of 'employability,' i.e. individuals' capability of gaining and maintaining employment, thus stressing their ability to be self-sufficient actors that draw on an appropriate set of skills, experiences and attitudes. A reason as to why some groups of the working population are excluded from the regular labor market is because of the fact that they are considered 'unhealthy,' 'disabled,' or in some other way 'unfit for work.' Hence, not only is this group of individuals seen as lacking in certain skills and abilities, their shortcomings also concern their health. Rather than turning this trend around, the increased significance of the health promotion discourse in contemporary working life may fuel this development by changing norms of 'employability.' The discourse's inclination to treat individuals' lifestyles and personal characteristics as key features of their health, well-being and employability, implies that 'unhealthy lifestyles,' 'passivity' and a general inability to manage oneself, may become signs not only of illness or disability, but also of un-employability.

2 Management and Health

As noted by Barker (1993: 409), 'control' has been a central concept in organizational theory for a long time and remains a key issue "that shapes and permeates our experiences of organizational life." In his seminal study, Edwards (1979) elucidated three types of workplace control that have been implemented to manage workers and their behavior and attitudes: (a) simple control; (b) technical control; and (c) bureaucratic control. These are presented in historical sequence, although remnants of the old control practices coexist with the new. 'Control' was defined as the "ability of capitalists and/or managers to obtain desired work behavior from workers. Such ability exists in greater or lesser degrees, depending upon the relative strength of workers and their bosses" (Edwards, 1979: 17).

What is interesting for our purposes is that these models of control are claimed to commonly result in such experiences as dependency, incapacity, lack of motivation and disengagement that have been seen to have negative effects on people's health and well-being (Green *et al.*, 2000; Parish, 1995; Koelen and van den Ban, 2004). In contrast to these traditional modes of control, the currently popular 'concertive' control strategy that is based on the idea of generating involvement, activity, enthusiasm and commitment among people, is said to empower employees and positively affect their health and well-being (Friedman, 2008a: 2008b; Luthans, 2002; Sonnenstuhl, 1986). In this chapter, we will discuss each model with a view of their alleged consequences for employee health and well-being. This discussion provides the foundation for the main argument of the next chapter, which revolves around the idea that popular worksite health promotion practices among employers can be seen as mechanisms of control, i.e. management.

TRADITIONAL MODES OF CONTROL AND 'NEGATIVE HEALTH'

According to Edwards the earliest type, traditional or 'simple control' existed when work was organized and controlled in a very direct and hands-on manner, on an ad hoc and arbitrary basis by supervisors and foremen. The

simple mode of control created a work environment characterized by inse-
curity, leading to stress and fatigue among employees (Polanyi *et al.*, 2000).
People were 'bossed around' and were subject to arbitrary decisions and
actions, grounded in managers' subjective viewpoints and impulses. Managers cast a long shadow over the operations, reducing workers' ability to
develop (Hanson, 2007). For sure, actions were taken to positively affect
employees' health and well-being in terms of social projects such as recreation and leisure activities (see Barley and Kunda, 1992). In line with other
activities they remained, however, unsystematic and temporary, thus reducing
the ability to have any positive long-term impact. Overall, the mechanisms
for achieving control were "very unsophisticated, and the system of control
tended to be informal and unstructured. The personal power and authority
of the capitalist constituted the primary mechanism for control." The capitalist, i.e. the manager,

> supervised the work activities directly; he maintained a close watch on
> his foremen; and he interceded immediately with full power to solve any
> problems, overriding established procedures, firing recalcitrant workers,
> recruiting new ones, rearranging work schedules, reducing pay, handling
> out bonuses, and so forth.
>
> (Edwards, 1979: 25)

In describing this kind of control, Edwards referred to 'the entrepreneurial
firm,' where operations were seen to be unstructured and where all power
and authority was vested in the owner/ entrepreneur.

> This use of power tended to undermine the exercise of routinized
> and formally organized power. Indeed, this was the advantage of
> entrepreneurial control in the small firm—the capitalist could intervene
> personally at all levels and in all activities to facilitate production.
>
> (Edwards, 1979: 26)

Edwards's ideas on simple control have some resemblances to Weber's
(1978: 241) "charismatic authority," where the ability to exercise power is
based on a person's extraordinary character. "These are such as are not
accessible to the ordinary person, but are regarded as of divine origin or as
exemplary, and on the basis of them the individual concerned is treated as a
'leader'." The term 'charisma' is applied to a certain quality of an individual
personality by virtue of which he or she is considered extraordinary and
treated with exceptional powers and qualities. As is the case of the entrepreneur, the charismatic person is deeply hostile to the existing order that he
or she seeks to change in a fundamental sense, thus challenging routines
and traditions. Eventually, however, charismatic domination will become
"routinized," i.e. taking on a more formal and organized character: "Indeed,
in its pure form charismatic authority may be said to exist only *in statu*

nascendi. It cannot remain stable, but becomes either traditionalized or rationalized, or a combination of both" (Weber, 1978: 246). In a similar vein, Edwards (1979: 30–31) referred to "the expanded firm" and "hierarchical control," marking "the firm's first accommodation to its growth." Under this regime, control remains 'simple' in the sense that "each boss—whether a foreman, supervisor, or manager—would re-create in his shop the situation of the capitalist under entrepreneurial control," thus substituting 'a capitalist's empire' with a 'supervisor's empire.' In this world, workers are reduced to puppets and their welfare is generally ignored (Barley and Kunda, 1992). Although regulated in the sense that a line of order and hierarchy is established,

> each boss would have full rights to fire and hire, intervene in production, direct workers as to what to do and what not to do, evaluate and promote or demote, discipline workers, arrange rewards, and so on; in short, each boss would be able to act in the same arbitrary, idiosyncratic, unencumbered way that entrepreneurs had acted.
>
> (Edwards, 1979: 31)

Certainly the basis for their domination is not their unique and extra-ordinary character in the Weberian sense, but a crude and raw hierarchy, where power is directly sanctioned by the owner. They could "never really re-create entrepreneurial control, because, unlike true entrepreneurs, foremen and supervisors under hierarchical control were not their own bosses" (Edwards, 1979: 32). In essence, hierarchical control, following the basic principles of simple control, has come to be known as 'close' supervision:

> Orders were received from the level above and transmitted to the levels below. The foreman directed operations by giving instructions and commands and by checking on work. Compliance was achieved because foremen exercised the capitalist's power, especially the power to punish or fire workers.
>
> (Edwards, 1979: 34)

The second type of control, "technical control," emerged from attempts to 'rationalize' the new assembly line; specifically by "designing machinery and planning the flow of work to minimize the problem of transforming labour power into labour as well as to maximize the purely physically based possibilities for achieving efficiencies" (Edwards, 1979: 112). Edwards described how technical control brought severe health-related consequences for the affected workers, primarily the high speed of work. But increased speed was not the only issue.

> With machinery driven at a uniform rate, workers could no longer create their own work rhythms. Independent spinners and weavers, just

like farmers, coopers, shoemakers, and other workers, tended to produce in spurts, working furiously for a while and then slacking off or
even stopping entirely to rest. Now, the machine-established pace was
uniform.

(Edwards, 1979: 114)

Continuing mechanization eroded the need for unique skills among workers,
"making the workforce more uniformly composed of unskilled and semi-
skilled machine operatives" (Edwards, 1979: 126). To some extent, Edward's
notion of technical control has similarities to Taylor's (1998) ideas on
"scientific management," where all employees, including foremen and
supervisor become technically regulated. In a famous statement, Taylor
claimed that "in the past the man has been first; in the future the system
must be first" (1998: iv). People are to work in a standardized, technically
controlled way. Neither the subjective viewpoints of employees, nor of
supervisors should direct the work that is to be carried out. Instead,
"scientific principles" should guide all employees' behavior. Taylor was
critical of the inefficiency of the traditional, 'simple' system that was based
on arbitrary rule of thumb.

Each man should daily be taught by and received the most friendly help
from those who are over him, instead of being, at the one extreme,
driven or coerced by his bosses, and at the other left to his own unaided
devices.

(Taylor, 1998: 10)

In his seminal study Braverman (1974) sparked interest in how the social
control of work resulting from Taylor's principles and its more contemporary adaptations fragment work and "deskill" workers, thus seriously
affecting their welfare and well-being (Nettleton and Bunton, 1995). "Under
scientific management the organization of work was to be the exclusive
responsibility of managers. There was thus a separation between those who
did the work and those who designed it" (Procter, 2005: 466). In this world,
individuals are to react, not to act and the employee is generally seen as an
instrument who is to execute orders without developing his or her intellectual and social abilities. Needless to say, this resulted in a host of health
problems such as alcoholism, depression and fatigue (Sonnenstuhl, 1986).
To this extent, technical control has close resemblances to simple control in
the sense that employees' own ideas and viewpoints are degraded or even
ignored.

The very first requirement for a man who is fit to handle pig-iron as a
regular occupation is that he shall be so stupid and so phlegmatic that
he more nearly resembles in his mental make-up the ox than any other
type. The man who is mentally alert and intelligent is for this very

reason entirely unsuited for what would, for him, be a grinding monotony of work of this character.

(Taylor, 1998: 59)

In a certain sense, workers become all the more competent by doing the same thing over and over again according to standardized principles. On the other hand, they gradually lose the ability to think in new and unexpected ways that may come from the acquisition of new experience. In this sense, previously competent and skilled workers are eventually replaced by unskilled or semi-skilled workers who are easy to hire and fire. This problem was acknowledged already by Adam Smith (1994: 429–30) in his studies of industrial production in England during the eighteenth century. He noted that a worker in an industrial organization that day in and day out effected a prescribed set of operations much according to Tayloristic principles "has no occasion to exert his understanding, or to exercise his invention and generally becomes as stupid and ignorant as it is possible for a human creature to become." Becoming a specialist comes "at the expense of his intellectual, social, and martial virtues." These problems are also related to the strict separation in bureaucratic organizations (see later) between those who do the work and those who design it. Critics have argued that bureaucracies offer few occasions for learning and growth beyond the immediate requirements of the specified work.

Overall, a key idea to both technical control in Edwards's sense and Tayloristic scientific management is the development of more rational methods for managing the shopfloor. Automation is one part of that enterprise, but this is not all there is to it. Taylor insisted that a "mental revolution" was needed among employers since they had become far too accustomed to managing by caprice. "Thus for Taylor, scientific management was more a way of thinking than a set of techniques, however crucial these might be" (Barley and Kunda, 1992: 371). The technically regulated control assumed, much in line with a simple mode of control, that workers should merely execute what they were told, without taking any individual initiatives. Negative health in terms of fatigue, stress and physical degradation among workers has been a standing theme in analyses of this control system (Hanson, 2007; Wilkinson, 1999). Learning and training should not come from any individual trial-and-error, but from a standardized and technically rational system that allowed the worker to perform certain operations only. "With scientific management the workman is not allowed to use whatever implements and methods he sees fit in the daily practice of his work" (Edwards, 1979: 67).

Eventually, technical control yielded to 'bureaucratic control'—a system developed essentially during the post-1945 period and that has been dominating much organization of businesses ever since. Bureaucracy's emergence as the preferred form of organization occurred, however, with the early rise of capitalism and the concomitant need to ensure impersonal, rational-legal transactions. Bureaucratic organizations are commonly said to handle the various demands of capitalist production more efficiently. Essentially, by routinizing all of the functions of management in the way that technical control had routinized the first function, bureaucratic control institutionalized the exercise of hierarchical power within organizations. Capitalist power was to be exercised through enacted rules and procedures. Bureaucratic control, like technical control, differs from simple control in that it grows out of the formal structure of the firm, rather than simply emanating from the personal relationships between workers and managers. Edwards stressed that

> while technical control is embedded in the physical and technological aspects of production and is built into the design of machines and the industrial architecture of the plant, bureaucratic control is embedded in the social and organizational structure of the firm and is built into job categories, work rules, promotion procedures, discipline, wage scales, definitions of responsibilities, and the like.
>
> (1979: 131)

Comprehensive systems of defining work tasks, directing workers and supervising and evaluating workers' performance were elaborated that had previously existed on a small scale only.

The defining features of bureaucracy sharply distinguish it from other types of control based on non-legal forms of authority. Weber (1978: 975) observed that the advantage of bureaucracy was that it was the most technically proficient form of organization, possessing specialized expertise, certainty, continuity and unity. "Bureaucracy develops the more perfectly, the more it is 'dehumanized,' the more completely it succeeds in eliminating from official business love, hatred, and purely personal, irrational, and emotional elements which escape calculation." Other characteristics of modern bureaucracy include its detached impersonality, rule-following, concentration of the means of administration, a levelling effect on social and economic differences and implementation of a system of authority that is practically indestructible: "Once fully established, bureaucracy is among those social structures which are the hardest to destroy" (ibid: 987). The process of bureaucratization suggests the possibility for carrying out specialized administrative functions according to purely objective considerations, where calculable rules stand at the center of attention. A central idea in Weber's thinking on bureaucracies is that any bureaucracy is a complex of social interaction of individual persons, i.e.

> there is no such thing as a collective personality which 'acts.' When reference is made in a sociological context to a state, a nation, a corporation, a family, or to similar collectivities, what is meant is, on the

contrary, *only* a certain kind of development of actual or possible social actions of individual persons.

(Weber, 1978: 14)

The various individuals' activities are oriented to a belief that there exists or should exist rules that are legitimate, hence authoritarian.

The individual in the bureaucracy is, ideally, "the personally detached and strictly objective *expert*" (Weber, 1978: 975). His or her activities are bounded by rules and operate within a specified sphere of competence. Individuals are "personally free and subject to authority only with respect to their impersonal official obligations" (ibid: 220). There is thus a strict hierarchical office authority; but outside the office, the individual is free to do as he or she pleases. In this sense,

> the emergence of the bureaucratic form of organization was predicated on a major anthropological innovation (that is, a new way of conceiving humanity and institutionally embedding it) that we have tended to take for granted these days, namely, the clear and institutionally supported separation of work from the rest of people's lives.
>
> (Kallinikos, 2003: 614)

The idea of 'office' as a distinct sphere of social life, has had an important significance for the constitution of modern society. The "zone of acceptance," i.e. the ability for the organization to exercise influence on the individual (Simon, 1997: 10), is seen to be limited to the office that the person occupies. It is only 'the official' that is being organized; hence the relevance of the widely accepted idea in organization theory of "partial inclusion" (see, e.g. Weick, 1969: 46). If, however, most aspects of a person's activities are undertaken according to the bureaucracy's rules and regulations, a relatively large section of an individual's identity can be said to be under the control of the bureaucracy. Such behaviors are often (but not necessarily) associated with what Weber (1978: 1375) names *Anstalt*, i.e. organizations such as mental hospitals, churches and prisons, but also large corporations, universities and government agencies (see, e.g. Davies, 1989; Perry, 1974; Shenkar, 1996; Stark, 1994; Tracy, 2000). In these organizations, distinctions between 'a private self' and a 'bureaucratic self' can be hard to make; still the general idea is that all bureaucrats act in a non-personal, hence impartial way, without involvement of any private feelings or emotions. They are only subject to authority as officials that enact certain roles (e.g. as prisoners, teachers, patients); not as private persons. Even in the face of harsh repression from the bureaucratic system, there is always the possibility to resist by not fully accepting 'the rules of the game.'

Critics of bureaucracies have argued that the true bureaucracy create alienation, i.e. a lack of commitment, dedication and devotion to the prescribed task to be carried out. Eventually, the alienated person may become sick, a reason as to why, for instance, emotional health programs grew substantially during the postwar years in the wake of proliferating bureaucratic organizations (see Sonnenstuhl, 1986). As described by, for instance, Whyte (1956) in his comments on "the organization man," or by Mills (1951) in his analysis of 'white collars,' the bureaucrat becomes an emotionally detached person, lacking in involvement and participation, hardly doing what is formally requested from him or her, which according to today's norm of activity and commitment would be seen as signs of 'unhealthiness' (Dean, 1995). Irrespective of the degree of involvement, the bureaucrat tends to become an expert within his or her limited area of competence, adding to the re-production of the bureaucracy's overall competence and expertise. Eventually, he or she may become 'stuck' in the organized machinery:

> The individual bureaucrat cannot squirm out of the apparatus into which he has been harnessed ... [T]he professional bureaucrat is chained to his activity in his entire economic and ideological existence. In the great majority of cases he is only a small cog in a ceaselessly moving mechanism which prescribes him an essentially fixed route of march.
>
> (Weber, 1978: 987–88)

This 'behavioral lock-in' is the result of experiential learning where the trained expert gradually establishes feedback between experience and competence, thus becoming all the more specialized but also simple-minded and myopic, unable to act in any other way than according to prescribed rules and routines even in the face of radically altered circumstances that should evoke a different response than the standard one (Levinthal and March, 1993). This unanticipated consequence of specialization has been seen as a major dysfunction of bureaucracies (see March and Simon, 1993; Merton, 1940). The "bureaucratization of the mind," says von Mises (1944: 81ff), kills ambition and destroys initiative. The end result is people who passively react to instructions and enact a world that is consistent with those (Argyris and Schön, 1996).

To sum up, *simple control* is the direct, authoritarian and personal control of work processes by a company's owner. Although widespread during the early 1900s, this philosophy still exists today in small family-owned companies, or during the early start-up phases of entrepreneurial corporations. It is claimed to create negative health effects due to the arbitrariness and the subjective grounds on which authority rests. *Technological control* prevails when most control emerges from the physical work environment, such as an assembly line; but also when work is closely regulated according to technical specifications and details. Critics have stressed the degrading character of 'Tayloristic' work, where employees' health and well-being gradually erodes. *Bureaucratic control*, the most familiar and widespread mode of control, relies on hierarchically-based social relations and rational-legal rules that reward compliance and loyalty. In terms of health and well-being, alienation remains a critical issue. A central idea to simple, technical and bureaucratic control is that they attend primarily to the behavior of people. As noted by March and Simon (1993: 12–39), a machine metaphor prevails, where the individual is seen to act as an instrument according to either the whims of an entrepreneur, the design of a technical environment, or established rules and procedures. Barker (1993: 410) noted that "control in the bureaucratic organization becomes impersonal because its authority rests ultimately with the system, leaving organization members, in many cases, with what Weber [1958: 182] called 'specialists without spirit, sensualists without heart'." Overall, simple control, technical control and bureaucratic control have operated on a principle of "requiring workers' labour power but formally sidelining their brain power and initiative," thus creating "high dissatisfaction, boredom, alienation, and low self-esteem" (Smith, 1997: 317), all well known as factors that deteriorate people's health and well-being (Hanson, 2007; Tones and Green, 2004).

NEW MANAGERIAL PRACTICES AND 'POSITIVE HEALTH'

The idea of winning the hearts and minds of the workforce, thus substituting 'harsh' and explicit modes of control with more subtle and implicit systems, have, however, eventually gained ground, not at least as the result of the debates in the US that were sparked by Lillian Gilbreth and Henry Gantt during the early decades of the twentieth century, who advocated the need for corporations to pay more attention to 'human factors,' particularly people's health and welfare. It was the work by Mayo and his colleagues Roethlisberger and Dickson on "human relations" that generated a more profound critique to dominating control strategies. Mayo (1933: 172) who had an explicit interest in the individual health and well-being of workers stressed that a problem of dispassion, low working morale and anomie characterized both governmental and industrial organizations. Therefore,

> it is no longer possible for an administrator to concern himself narrowly with his special function and to assume that the controls established by a vigorous social code will continue to operate in other areas of human life and action.
>
> (Mayo, 1933: 172)

According to Mayo and his colleagues, workers' attitudes, sentiments and emotions need to be taken into account, in order to secure good collaboration on the shop floor, happiness and well-being that would ultimately result in high productivity. Managers must become "good listeners"; they must take into account the viewpoints and ideas of employees. They must also understand the importance of creating a good working environment that can contribute to workers' motivation, commitment and the strengthening of their mental and physical health.

Based in the human relations school, a host of 'human-oriented' approaches have been developed. As a critique of the simple, technical and bureaucratic systems of control, new modes of control emphasize the 'empowerment' of workers that are said to increase their commitment and well-being. Organizations are:

> increasingly looking for more than obedience. Instead of encouraging subordination, they are promoting 'empowerment.' They are searching for ways to motivate people to invent new things, to make the old rules obsolete. This demands a less hierarchical relationship than traditional loyalty.
>
> (Heckscher, 1995: 7)

This approach has gained popularity as traditional industries based on primarily bureaucratic control, have encountered problems in a harsh global world; and where instead allegedly innovation-driven, flexible and 'agile' organizations have become the masters of the scene. Eventually,

> manufacturing work settings defined by standardization, hierarchy, constraint and the curtailment of workers' input would give way to new sociotechnical systems in which workers would be empowered to become pattern-finders and problem-solvers, to learn from their errors, and to deploy and redeploy machines for a multiplicity of purposes. Fluidity, a climate for ongoing learning and meaningful participation could be imported into the corporate, white-collar world of work as well, providing a foundation for a more integrated, non-hierarchical, and innovative work environment.
>
> (Smith, 1997: 318)

Overall, the end of classic control strategies and the rise of flexible modes of organization has been prophesized since at least the early signs of post-industrialism were reported by Bell (1973). Initial contributions in managerial theory saw the pursuit of flexible organization as a one-dimensional and commendable process: work was to be handled within informally constituted teams, which were formed to deal with temporary projects, and which were coordinated by shared values and trust-based relations (e.g. Halal, 1994; Heckscher and Donnellon, 1994). Such characterization has been seen to imply fundamental changes in the nature of managerial work and in the principles and techniques of controlling employees. In essence, employees are not said to be controlled but empowered to work in teams in relation to which managers orchestrated rather than managed (Mintzberg, 1998). This need is seen to be particularly acute given the idea in much contemporary management literature that the traditional differentiation of person from role or office is outdated (Höpfl, 2006). In order to completely and fully energize individuals in the new, global and boundaryless economy, employees' selves become part of corporate regulation and control (Grey and Garsten, 2001).

Overarching this development,

> is the tenet of 'Continuous Improvement.' No limits to production can be allowed to remain static but should always be tested and pushed back. Once one problem has been dealt with, it will reveal other problems which must be addressed.
>
> (Sewell and Wilkinson, 1992: 278)

In this world, employees must be active and entrepreneurial, and any control system must be designed in a way to foster these characteristics. Within a framework of shared values and norms, employees must be allowed to take actions, to correct errors, to 'think outside the box,' to challenge professional roles, organizational constituencies and traditions. According to Barker (1993: 411–12), this can be seen as an illustration to "concertive control strategies" that represents a key shift in the locus of control from management to the workers themselves, "who collaborate to develop the means of their own control." This can, for instance, occur in self-managing teams that operate according to principles of continuous improvement, thus manifesting "the transformation of a traditional, hierarchically based organization to a flat confederation of concretively controlled self-managing teams." As Barker suggested, proponents of self-managing teams argue that they make companies more productive, "by letting workers manage themselves in small, responsive, highly committed, and highly productive groups."

Indeed, for at least two decades, the management literature has been filled with calls for efforts to strengthen employees' motivation, commitment and involvement, rather than to seek traditional managerial controls. For instance, Walton (1985: 77–79), making a conceptual difference between a "control strategy" to work, and a "commitment strategy," argued that:

> workers respond best—and most creatively—not when they are tightly controlled by management, placed in narrowly defined jobs, and treated like an unwelcome necessity, but, instead, when they are given broader responsibilities, encouraged to contribute, and helped to take satisfaction in their work.

He stressed the importance of encouraging participation by everyone, and "to create jobs that involve greater responsibility and more flexibility" that would enact a "new commitment-based approach."

As a consequence of global capitalism and the concomitant requirements on employers to be innovation-driven, knowledge-intensive, flexible and open to continuous learning and change, employees must be given the opportunity to constantly develop their skills and abilities in order to become 'entrepreneurial.' Brousseau *et al.* (1996: 52) noted that organizations are making abundant changes internally to cope with a highly turbulent external environment. "With frequent reorganizing, downsizing, rightsizing, delayering, flattening the pyramid, teaming and outsourcing taking place, careers and career opportunities are in pandemonium resulting from the progressive destabilization of relationships between people and organizations." They concluded that responsibility for career development must be given to the individual, not the organization;

> individuals should prepare themselves for a career involving frequent changes in employers and in the very nature of the work that they perform. People need to be more flexible and versatile in their skills and knowledge, and must be willing to go anywhere, at any time, and at a moment's notice, to do anything.
>
> (Brousseau *et al.*, 1996: 52)

In essence, and in significant contrast to previous modes of control, the worker should be given the opportunity to act responsibly, independently and take initiative; he or she should be encouraged to become an 'enterprising self' (Du Gay *et al.*, 1996). According to this view, flexible social skills are seen as significant career tools for the individual employee. In this way, the shift away from bureaucracy implies that people cannot rely as much on directives. Rather, they are seen to be the authors of their own work.

Numerous scholars have argued that the 'active and healthy employee' is intimately linked to the idea of the 'post-bureaucratic organization' (see Costea *et al.*, 2007; Heckscher, 1994). By way of its decentralized, loosely coupled, flexible, nonhierarchical and fluid structure, this kind of organization offers the institutional context to strengthening one's health by becoming energetic, flexible and autonomous. Indeed, in recent years an increasing number of works have pointed to the demise of the bureaucratic organization and the emergence of a new post-bureaucratic form of organization— referred to as the entrepreneurial or networked-shaped organization where strong organizational values rather than formal rules play a vital role. In the managerial discourse, post-bureaucracies are typically seen to offer a positive break with the bureaucratic legacy—they are explicitly 'anti-bureaucratic' (e.g. Baker, 1992; Bartlett and Ghoshal, 1997; Peters, 1992; Savage, 1996). Instead of alienation, social integration is offered that is regarded as critical to maintain and strengthen people's well-being (Hanson, 2007). Weberian bureaucracies with its focus on rules and regulations, fixed boundaries, rigid division of labor and strict hierarchical control systems, are seen as mechanisms of oppression, which degrade human dignity and inhibit emancipation and empowerment. Moreover, they appear sluggish and incapable of flexible change that are said to characterize today's global competition. As already said, it is claimed that bureaucracies' ways of constraining individual freedom also create functional limitations. The hierarchical and impersonal structures of bureaucracies are said to create passive and inflexible people, unable to handle contemporary societies' swiftly changing requirements and demands. In contrast, the flat and organic structures of post-bureaucracies make employees creative and capable of molding themselves to the variety of new problems and challenges they face (Adler, 2001; Benveniste, 1994). By empowering people, putting them at the center of attention, strengthening their commitment and motivation, they are a true manifestation of some of the main principles of the human relations movement's focus on individuals' welfare and well-being.

In the post-bureaucratic organization 'organizational culture' rather than explicit rules, standard operating procedures and regulations have emerged as the main means of control. Indeed, the notion of organizational culture has gained much attention as a mechanism for creating committed, motivated and healthy employees (see Conrad and Walsh, 1992). Barley and Kunda (1992: 382) have suggested that organizational culture is a new managerial ideology that seeks to promote the devotion and commitment among employees who are seen as vital features when organizations became all the more network-like, i.e. characterized by lateral and horizontal interlinkages (e.g. Davidow and Malone, 1992; Savage, 1996); project-based in the sense of designing work tasks into distinct temporal phases (Hodgson, 2004); when they introduce flatter structures and reduced hierarchy according to management models of 'Total Quality Management,' 'Just in Time,' 'Lean Production' and 'Business Process Reengineering'; when they institute workplace programs of quality circles, job enlargement and rotation, and the promulgation of a new ethos of participation; or when they become 'virtual' in the sense of acquiring a 'boundaryless' character. In these 'post-bureaucratic entities,' it is popularly claimed, organizational culture has the potential to foster increased responsibility and commitment among individuals by outlining critical values and norms to which people feel strong loyalty. Specifically, these organizational arrangements stress the capability of people for managing themselves by appealing to their underlying experiences, thoughts and feelings that guide their actions.

According to Kunda (1992: 11–12), this logic emphasizes that members act in the best interest of the organization as "they are driven by internal commitment, strong identification with company goals, intrinsic satisfaction from work," thus stressing "a growing managerial interest in psychological absorption of workers by organizations." This kind of control is more comprehensive and extensive than simple, technical and bureaucratic means of authority, where domains of the self once considered private come under corporate scrutiny and regulation: "What one does, thinks, or feels—indeed, *who one is*—is not just a matter of private concern but the legitimate domain of bureaucratic control structures armed with increasingly sophisticated techniques of influence" (ibid: 13–14, emphasis added). In essence, this kind of control can be seen as an appeal to the potential existing in people including their health and well-being:

> To the extent that they are shaped, that shaping is framed as a process of education, personal development, growth, and maturity—in fact, a development of a better, healthier self, saved from the threat of anomie and alienation and the pathology of conflict.
>
> (Kunda, 1992: 14)

Thus, the post-bureaucratic organization stresses the idea that people are no longer only responsible for how they carry out their specified jobs; but also how they contribute to a larger whole, including their lifestyles.

> The master concept is *an organization in which everyone takes responsibility for the success of the whole.* If that happens, then the basic notion of regulating relations among people by *separating* them into specific, predefined functions must be abandoned. The problem is to create a system in which people can enter relations that are determined by problems rather than predetermined by the structure. Thus, organization control must centre not on the management of tasks but the management of relationships; in effect 'politics' must be brought into the open.
>
> (Heckscher, 1994: 24)

This argument stresses that management and control is about governing work through caring about the lifestyle, health and well-being of people.
Costea *et al.* stressed that

> only if human subjects intensify their contributions *as selves* can they (as human resources) enhance the production process and lead the organization to success. The omnipresent slogan 'people are our most important asset' is much deeper than the episodic waxing and waning of one fashion or another.
>
> (2007: 246)

The 'self' stands at the center of controlling work, emphasizing such notions as 'excellence,' 'skills,' 'performance,' 'commitment,' 'wellness,' 'health' and 'creativity.' The link between increased personal engagement and effective production is regarded as key, where all aspects of the self belong and are taken care of:

> The novelty of the intensive appropriation of subjectivity by managerialism lies in the representation of work as a process of releasing the

full potentialities of the self, as a locus in which self-exploration and expression are encouraged, as a place where traditional restrictive controls recede into the background.

(Costea *et al.*, 2007: 253)

Traditional modes of control are

replaced by a new style of engagement in which self-expression is encouraged while control is situated in the processes of self-examination, evaluation and reflection. In other words, the site of control is also displaced to a significant extent from external authority to inner attributes of the subject who is urged to self-manage.

(Costea *et al.*, 2007: 253)

This marks a subtle twist in the cultural dynamic of managerial control by "encouraging autonomous employees to use their alleged independence to express their resourcefulness as well as to submit themselves to continuous self-scrutiny and audit in the name of accountability" (Costea *et al.*, 2007: 253). In an organizational world where the 'self' is placed at the center of the employee–employer relationship, it becomes captured by practices of self-improvement and self-development, i.e. self-management. A critical issue remains the continuous improvement of a healthy self, of discovering a better self, or a better way of being oneself, thus emphasizing the idea that "human subjectivity becomes the central resource of production" (ibid: 260).

A recent and prominent example of this ideology of control is Stewart Friedman's suggestions on "total leadership," which argues that people can improve their performance in multiple domains of their lives—work, home, community and self—by learning to lead more effectively in all of them. Friedman has published his suggestions in the paper "Learning to Lead in all Domains of Life" (Friedman, 2006), in the book *Total Leadership: Be a Better Leader, Have a Richer Life* (Friedman, 2008a), as well as in a paper with a similar title (Friedman, 2008b). In the following, it is the paper from 2006 that is used as a reference. A core idea is that to be an efficient leader (which is not limited to people officially holding executive positions) you need to consider all domains of your life, acting as a "whole person" as opposed to a leader at work that is isolated from life's other domains. Friedman (2006) argues that the business environment of the twenty-first century requires that "we view leadership and life as pieces of the same puzzle," integrating work, home, community and self and where the goal is to "increase business results by enriching lives." The total leadership (TL) approach is said to be centered on self-designed and self-directed leadership, where participants are highly committed, engaged and vigilant about their health and well-being. A fundamental idea is that "no longer is business leadership limited to top executives; it is expected at all levels." Hence, all employees should act as leaders, i.e. as active, strong, motivated, creative and committed actors. This is seen to be particularly important in the post-bureaucratic era, where it is 'up to you' to promote your career and personal development.

> Through the TL process, participants take the opportunity to change the meaning of leadership in their own lives. Their identities as leaders change: They increase the degree to which they see themselves as leaders capable of demonstrating authenticity, integrity, and creativity.
>
> (Friedman, 2006: 1273)

The TL approach that is about "driving performance and improving results" is said to start with "your life as a whole—your life at work, your life at home, your life in the community, and your own health and spirit." By acting according to certain TL "principles and skills," people will "learn to think in new and creative ways by adopting an experimental mind-set, and they acquire new skills for demonstrably improving results at work, at home, in the community, and for their own health and spirit." The strategy is said to build both commitment and accountability that are regarded as critical success factors in organizations that are less hierarchical than ever before, generating ambiguous internal relationships and manifesting diverse stakeholder interests. Three principles are said to provide the conceptual basis for the TL approach: (a) clarify what's important; (b) recognize and respect the whole person; and (c) continually experiment with how goals are achieved. The first principle is about articulating a vision that embraces the values and lifestyles of employees and making sure that these are aligned to "the core values of the business." Through continual observation and reflections, employees are to "know their priorities, strengths, and weaknesses." They should "strive to increase commitment to shared goals" and to "hold themselves and others accountable for pursuing valued goals." The second principle is about taking responsibility for respecting the value of all aspects of one's life and nurturing "networks and partnerships that provide the support needed for achieving results that matter." The third principle stresses that "effective leaders continually rethink the means by which work gets done in ways that force a results-driven focus and provide maximum flexibility with choice in how, when, and where things get done." People should have "the requisite courage and openness to experiment with new work methods and communication tools to better meet performance expectations."

In a review of Friedman's ideas in the scholarly journal *Human Resource Management*, Ollier-Malaterre (2009) describe them as a "bold vision of leadership," illustrating a typical view of American positive thinking, "which emphasizes individual freedom over fate and encourages the challenging of social expectations." According to Ollier-Malaterre, "in that sense, it is highly energizing and liberating." An article in *The New York Times* (2008) states:

> "Mr Friedman's philosophy is fairly straightforward. The fundamental premise is that leadership can exist in every person, whether at the top, middle or bottom of any group" and that "leadership should not be confined to work, but extended to one's personal life, community involvement and family life."
>
> (*The New York Times*, 2008)

It is concluded that "experts in the leadership field say that today's business climate is especially conducive to a type of leadership informed by strong personal values," where authenticity and looking at the whole person stands at the center. One person interviewed who previously had participated in one of Friedman's courses acknowledged in the article that "in the end, it wasn't just about how I could do better at work ... It is holistic." At the webpage www.totalleadership.org a host of articles and videos are presented that explain the principles of total leadership and the benefits that come from them in terms of increased individual productivity and well-being. In a speech, Stewart Friedman himself expresses that "now more than ever, your success as a leader isn't just about being a great businessperson. You've got to be a great person, performing well in all domains of your life" (*The New York Times*, 2008).

Friedman's ideas can effectively be placed in a context that emphasizes 'positive leadership' of oneself, and of others. These issues have recently been suggested by a number of management scholars that are part of a movement named 'positive organizational scholarship' that centers on (but is not limited to) the activities of the Center for Positive Organizational Scholarship at the University of Michigan (see http://www.bus.umich.edu/Positive/). During the last years, a number of papers relating to this research program have been published in organization and management journals, such as the *Journal of Organizational Behavior, Academy of Management Executive, Harvard Business Review, Organizational Dynamics, Journal of Management, Human Resource Development Review, Leadership and Organization Development Journal, Journal of Leadership* and *Organizational Studies, Journal of Management Inquiry*, to mention a few. A number of scholars have given fairly similar definitions of 'positive leadership,' and we need therefore not review all of them (see, e.g. Bernstein, 2003; Cameron and Caza, 2004; Luthans, 2002; Roberts, 2006). For instance, Caza and Caza (2008: 22) stressed that "organizational science is predominantly based on a deficit model of organizations in which problems are identified and corrected" and that "far less attention has focused on overtly positive processes and variables." They suggested that 'positive psychology' offers an analogy and "clarifies the important difference between enhancing the positive and eliminating the negative." Traditional clinical psychology is said to have focused on eliminating or curing illness, however neglecting how it should *create health*: "Anyone who has been in better physical condition than they are in now, or one who has recovered from prolonged illness, knows that there is a qualitative difference between not being sick and feeling healthy." The authors argued that organizations need not only eliminate problems; but must also focus on "increasing the positive." Hence, they should not only try to "fix what is wrong with managers and employees," but also focus on "people's strengths and psychological capabilities" (Luthans, 2002: 57). Cameron and Caza (2004: 731) stressed that this should lead to "exceptional individual and organizational performance, such as developing human strength, producing resilience and restoration, and fostering vitality." One of the main proponents of positive leadership, management scholar Robert Quinn recollected a telephone call by a professor at a medical school who had attended one of Mr Quinn's seminars. This man who had contacted Mr Quinn "thought he was in the business of helping veterans to recover from stress. If instead he sees himself in the business of helping veterans become optimal, functioning human beings, it's a really different story" (Bernstein, 2003: 269). Luthans (2002: 59–60) stressed that positive leadership is largely about people's 'self-efficacy,' i.e. one's ability to "produce desired results." In a concerted effort by a number of leading 'positive organizational scholars,' a claim was made in the *Harvard Business Review* that "every organization must filter out failing employees and ensure that everyone performs at an expected level of competence" (Roberts *et al.*, 2005: 1–2), which can be accomplished through a methodology called Reflected Best Self exercise that allows people "to develop a sense of their 'personal best' in order to increase their future potential." The "self-discovery process" that follows from this test, can help people to "develop a much broader and richer understanding of yourself," thus helping them to answer the question whether or not they can meet the expected requirements or if they should rather do something else. In another article by positive organization scholars published by *Organization Science,* Spreitzer *et al.* (2005: 537) introduced the concept of "thriving" in order to emphasize individuals' "experience of vitality and learning." It was claimed that thriving is an important mechanism of "self-adaptation," not only in the sense of how rational individuals exercise "self-observation, self-reward, and self-punishment as a way to regulate their own behavior," but also how they "self-regulate based on how they feel." In this sense, thriving "is likely to contribute to positive health."

In conclusion, in this chapter we have discussed the literature on organizational control to show how the specific principles and techniques of controlling employees in organizations have developed from the late nineteenth century up to the early twenty-first century. The review points toward three major transformations: from 'simple control' to 'technical control'; from 'technical control' to 'bureaucratic control'; and finally from 'bureaucratic control' to 'concertive control.' The discussion suggests, first, how these transformations have been accompanied by concerns not only for the efficiency of organizations; but also for the health and well-being of employees. Second, it suggests how organizational scholars have recently begun to explore an allegedly positive relationship between the concerns for organizational efficiency and the concerns for the health and well-being of employees. Whereas under the simple, technical or bureaucratic control regimes, it was generally assumed that organizational efficiency and employee health and well-being were at odds with one another, it is frequently assumed today that the concertive control regime affects employee health and well-being in a positive way. Third, our review suggests that whereas the simple, technical and bureaucratic control regimes all make a sharp distinction between the professional self and the private self of the employee; the concertive control regime differs from the other three in that it seeks to avoid making this distinction. This ambition of organizing 'the whole individual' centers on establishing 'a positive relationship' between organizational efficiency and employee health and well-being. In this sense a close connection can be found between contemporary regimes of organizational control and principles and techniques of health promotion.

3   Health Promotion as Management

In line with what was said in the previous chapter, the standard view of the health-management nexus is that individual health can be seen as the outcome of different management ideologies. The 'concertive' control strategy that is currently dominating management thinking and practice promises 'positive health' by unleashing human energy, commitment and engagement. However, as implied in Chapter 1 activities that explicitly aim to promote good health and well-being among employees can be understood as expressions of management in the sense of constituting particular loyalties, identities and subjectivities. In this sense, the pursuit of a 'healthy lifestyle' may not only be the result of a certain organizational environment and culture; but may in fact be a constituting feature of them. To this extent 'health' is a key mechanism of organized human behavior, i.e. management, where health promotion activities are the concrete practices through which a certain management ideology can be realized; specifically that of creating an active, self-managing and self-regulating individual who controls all aspects of his or her life.

In her book *The Imperative of Health* Lupton (1995: 70) noted that most of the literature on health promotion begins by attempting to define 'health.' Typically, students of health promotion put forward the World Health Organization's (WHO) definition of health as a state of complete physical, social and mental well-being, and not merely the absence of disease or infirmity (see WHO, 2010). Thus, according to standard definitions of health in the health promotion literature, 'health' denotes more than a medical condition, disease or lack thereof. Certainly according to this view, the official definitions and interpretations of 'health' rarely allow for individuals' own definitions of health. "For example, according to the WHO definition, people who are permanently disabled are not healthy, even though they may require little medical care or ongoing treatment" (Lupton, 1995: 72). Addressing this issue, Blaxter (1990: 13–15) reported that some students of health promotion have argued that the only valid measure of 'health' is to accept people's own assessment of whether they are healthy or not. Other researchers have claimed that the issue of what is 'health' must not be a topic for the lay person, but for the health promotion expert (see Parish, 1995).

Thorogood and Coombes argued that

> there are a wide variety of concepts of health that differ between individuals, between professions, and between cultures. At one end of a spectrum health is defined as the absence of disease or longevity and at the other end health is seen as the concept of enablement or wellbeing ... Just as health has many definitions, it is not surprising that health promotion is also defined in a number of ways.
>
> (2004: 3–4)

Responding to this issue Hanson (2007: 25–26) suggested that there are three ways of looking at initiatives that aim to address people's health: (a) treat illness; (b) prevent illness; and (c) promote health. He argued that when treating and preventing illness, "health becomes synonymous with the absence of illness" that can be confirmed through medical diagnosis. Promoting health, on the other hand, then 'health' is "something quite different from the absence of illness." According to this perspective, "it becomes more difficult to define exactly what health is." Hanson (2007: 54–55) concluded that health can be regarded as (a) "clinical status," i.e. health based on human physiology and anatomy; (b) "health as functional ability/capacity," i.e. health as one's ability to perform social duties; and (c) "health as wellbeing," i.e. a "person's overall experience of feeling well or unwell."

Koelen and van den Ban (2004: 26) stressed that "the question 'What is health?' seems to be a simple one, but the answer is not always straightforward. In itself it is difficult to define health in terms of objective, measurable criteria." Similarly Blaxter (1990: 3) argued that the concept of 'health' proposes a number of conceptual difficulties. Some diseases or physiological statuses can be identified and evaluated (though less easily in a large population such as at a worksite); but this is not the whole of health: "health and illness are social as well as biological facts." Hence, the definition and classification of disease, as well as health in the health promotion literature, relies to some extent on an idea of social construction by stressing its functional aspects: you are ill, when you cannot perform your social roles in the 'normal' fashion (see Parsons, 1951). You are healthy when you can do so (Blaxter, 1990: 36). Koelen and van den Ban (2004) maintained that "for centuries, health was defined in terms of the absence of physical disability. From this medical-biological point of view, persons for instance suffering from chronic diseases or a physical handicap were considered to be unhealthy" (2004: 26). They argued that today, however, health

> is looked at from a holistic point of view. It is a positive concept, expressed in functional terms. Health is not an end, but a means, a resource that enables people to lead an individually, socially and economically productive life.
>
> (Koelen and van den Ban 2004: 29–30)

Therefore, much emphasis is placed in the health promotion literature upon planning and coordination, assessing needs, consultation with the appropriate individuals and groups, piloting and evaluating programs. "The major focus in health promotional rhetoric is on fostering 'positive health,' preventing illness and disease rather than treatment" (Lupton, 1995: 51).

Arguing that health is "an elusive term because the state of being healthy can be viewed from a multitude of perspectives," Arnold and Breen (2006: 4–17) proposed a number of "images of health." One of these was "health as the antithesis of disease." As is typical in mainstream medical discourse, the authors claimed that, "when health is defined as the absence of disease, evaluative statements about clients are made within the parameters of illness, using a system of disease signs and symptoms." Another image was "health as growth," i.e. health as the successful achievement of certain tasks crucial to particular life stages. According to this view, "health is seen as being intimately determined by individual lifestyle and behavioral choices." As already implied, related to this approach is the image of "health as functionality," i.e. health as the ability to fulfill critical social and organizational functions: both physiological (digestion, sleep, hydration, etc.) and psychological (behavior, communication, emotional development, etc.). "Fulfillment of these functions defines a healthy individual." According to the image "health as goodness of fit," the authors emphasized the fit between the person and his or her environment. According to this perspective, individual lifestyle is said to have a crucial effect on one's health. A further image, according to Arnold and Breen was "health as wholeness," stressing a "holistic image of health" that implies that every aspect of a human being or social system interacts in a complex way, where the individual or social system is considered as a whole unity. "Health as wellbeing" is a view on health that builds on WHO's definition of health (see earlier). Obviously, 'well-being' is a highly subjective experience, linked to individuals' sense-making and emotions. The image "health as empowerment," stresses the idea that a healthy individual is an 'empowered individual,' i.e. a person who is able to take responsibility for his/her health and life in general. Finally, "health as resource" is an image which stresses that "health is competence; a well of strengths, some apparent and some unrecognized but all able to be cultivated and actualized." This view regards health as a role that can be learned and nurtured, indeed cultivated as an advanced skill. In a similar vein Quick *et al.* (2007: 193) suggested the following "attributes of healthy individuals":

Leading a life of purpose

Clear mission and goals
Balanced—living within one's value system
Integrity
Productive

Purposeful work
Spiritual or higher purpose basis
Passion or motivation to achieve for the better good

Quality connections to others

Interdependent: strong, positive social support system
Emotional competence
Mature, intimate connection to family and significant others
Communication competence

Positive self-regard and mastery

Humour
Hope and optimism
Self-efficacy or confidence
Self awareness—strength focus—a component of emotional competence
Subjective wellbeing/happiness
Hardiness, self-reliance, and adaptability
Vigour, physical and mental energy
Personal challenge and growth goals

Obviously, from these accounts, there are many ways of envisioning health in the health promotion literature. Therefore, "it is well recognized that concepts of *health* and *health promotion* are both essentially contested: their philosophical basis and the principles governing definitions and practice are all open to multiple interpretations" (Tones and Green, 2004: 1). "Health, like love, beauty or happiness, is a metaphysical concept, which eludes all attempts at objectivisation" (Skrabanek, 1994: 15). Thus, "like all linguistic practices, health is metaphorical—absorbing and expressing a range of meanings found throughout culture" (Crawford, 2006: 405).

DEFINING HEALTH PROMOTION

Certainly the idea of 'health promotion' is not new. In their overview of the field, Green *et al.* (2000) noted that many of the prevailing methods of community health in the nineteenth century had many of the political and ecological features of modern health promotion. But the history is longer than that: intellectual roots can be traced to antiquity. During the first half of the twenty-first century, attempts have been made to make health promotion a prominent feature of public health. As Parish (1995) noted, the term 'health promotion' was almost unknown until the late 1970s; but today it figures as a key policy issue in much national and international debate on social policy, work and employment.

One of the most important developments on the international scene during the 1970s was the publication of the Lalonde Report (Lalonde, 1974). Marc Lalonde was the Minister for Health and Welfare in Canada, and argued that too many resources were devoted to treating sickness, rather than preventing it. In brief, Lalonde stressed that society's focus of attention should not only be structural causes of bad health, but also people's lifestyles; their behaviors and attitudes. "This document stimulated international enthusiasm for health promotion as an approach to planning that could be potentially useful for governments, organizations, communities, and individuals" (Green *et al.*, 2000: 2–4), and it provided the impetus for health promotion programs in a number of countries. Within WHO, this initiated a discussion on how to promote health globally. The First International Conference on Health Promotion was held in 1986, which issued the Ottawa Charter for Health Promotion (see WHO, 1986). Today, the World Health Organization is one of the main proponents of health promotion, as witnessed by, e.g. the internationally endorsed *Health For All* program (WHO Regional Office for Europe, 2005). The most important document for the contemporary debate on health promotion remains, however, the Ottawa Charter, where health promotion is defined as "the process of enabling people to increase control over, and to improve, their health." The ideological claims implied by the Ottawa Charter can be given fundamentally different meanings in terms of political ideas; from Marxist positions on equity to conservative perspectives regarding individual responsibilities for health and well-being. Critics have argued that a common denominator of these perspectives is, however, states' attempts to free themselves of some of the responsibilities for people's health, where citizens are expected to manage their own health in a more committed and active way than before.

> Thus we have seen an intensification and generalization of the health-promotion strategies developed in the 20th century, coupled with the rise of a private health insurance industry, enhancing the obligations that individuals and families have for monitoring and managing their own health. Every citizen must now become an active partner in the drive for health, accepting their responsibility for securing their own well-being. Organizations and communities are also urged to take an active role in securing the health and well-being of their employees and members.
>
> (Rose, 2001: 6)

As is the case with the concept of 'health,' numerous definitions of health promotion exist in the mainstream health promotion literature. "When we speak of 'health promotion,' we are talking about the idea of helping people to move from their current state of health to a greater state of health" (Sloan *et al.*, 1987: 24). Crawford (2000: 220) defined health promotion as "the set of discourses and practices concerned with individual behaviors, attitudes, dispositions or lifestyle choices said to affect health." According to

Koelen and van den Ban (2004: 71) health promotion programs "are designed to stimulate individuals and groups to maintain healthy behaviors, to change unhealthy ones, or to adopt new behaviors conducive to health." In a similar vein, Downie *et al.* (1996: 2) argued that "health promotion comprises efforts to enhance positive health and reduce the risk of ill-health, through the overlapping spheres of health education, prevention, and health protection." Korp (2002: 71) suggested that one way of addressing the concept of 'health promotion' is to simply acknowledge its face value. Health promotion is to this extent all efforts dedicated to promote people's health. According to such a perspective, the term 'promote' means 'to maintain' or 'to improve' and the term 'health' implies all kinds of definitions, ranging from health as a clinical status to health as personal well-being. As Korp noted, this way of addressing health implies that you avoid defining health and health promotion, thus allowing for all kinds of activities that are said to contribute to individuals' 'health and well-being.' It implies a view on health as something unproblematic, good and positive—all efforts, as long as they are effective, to promote health are valuable and important. Thus, "'health promotion' as a term and concept is extremely broad, and could conceivably encompass any enterprise directed at 'promoting' 'health'" (Lupton, 1995: 50).

Downie *et al.* (1996: 1) maintained that the term 'health promotion' refers to a movement which has gathered momentum from the 1990s onward. It is a radical one which challenges traditional bio-medical definitions of health, "stresses its social and economic aspects, and portrays health as having a central place in a flourishing human life." Much of health promotion rhetoric is about challenging a dominant bio-medical perspective on health, by not primarily focusing on curing diseases, but rather on preventing sickness and promoting 'health.' The 'anti-authoritarian' flavor of health promotion is well illustrated by MacDonald (1998: 24) who, much like many other proponents of health promotion, criticized the growing power of the medical establishment over individuals' lives, stating that "this author resists any attempt to confer on the study of health promotion the status of a 'discipline' in its own right. May it never become expert-ridden!." This is in line with Bunton and Macdonald's (1992: 1) definition that stressed that as a discourse, health promotion has been drawing on a "social, as opposed to bio-medical model of health," emphasizing a "multi-focused approach" based on a "truly multi-disciplinary" enterprise. Seedhouse (1997: 1) commented on this by saying

> many of its devotees think of health promotion as the front line in the attack on a tired 'biomedical model' obsessed with disease and illness. Only the most radical health promoters are wholeheartedly set against medicine—most accept that clinicians have a place in the fight for health—but the great majority are opposed to (what they see as) the continuing medical dominance of health creation.

In this respect, Tones and Green (2004: 2) suggested an "empowerment model of health promotion" that "should operate as a kind of militant wing of public health," challenging clinical medicine's alleged power and paternalistic approach.

Hence, the health promotion discourse is generally seen as a close ally to the well-known medicalization critique. Literally, medicalization means "to make medical." According to *The Concise Oxford Dictionary* (1999: 885), to medicalize is to "treat as a medical problem, especially without justification." A standard definition of medicalization in sociological analyses is the process by which human behaviors become defined and treated as medical problems and issues (see, e.g. Ballard and Elston, 2005; Bull, 1990; Conrad, 2007). Zola (1972: 487) explained it as follows: "Making medicine and the labels 'healthy' and 'ill' *relevant* to an ever increasing part of human existence." Medicalization can be illustrated by the phenomenon of transforming such behaviors as menopause, eating disorder, suicide, infertility, melancholia, pedophilia, child abuse, impotence, criminality, hyperactivity, dying and childbirth into medical cases, thus turning them into legitimate issues for medical intervention and control. Although some behaviors seem more completely medicalized than others, a number of studies have stressed a considerable variety of human behavior that is increasingly being treated and organized as medical issues in terms of sickness and illness. In his "sick role theory," Parsons (1951) suggested that being sick or healthy is not necessarily a bio-medical status: as has already been said, it can also be regarded as a social role learned from experience. According to this perspective, a 'sick' person is not a unique personality, he or she is enacting a role provided to them by others, much as any other *homo sociologicus* would do. The role is linked to certain collective activities that are being reproduced by people carrying out their roles. A person acting as patient enacts certain organized activities, e.g. medical treatment. In that regard, the concept of medicalization is not primarily concerned with the 'objective' state of an organism as a biological system, but with experiential learning of social roles that are grounded in individual experience.

By emphasizing the social side of health, illness and related medical concepts to explain the increase in medical conditions among people in contemporary society, critics of medicalization, such as proponents of health promotion, have brought attention to how illness, health, disease and related 'personal conditions' are in fact created in medically-oriented social practices and are, as a consequence, sociological rather than bio-medical in character (Corker and Shakespeare, 2002; Thomas, 2002). As already suggested, the health promotion discourse seeks to challenge medicine's dominance, through a 'positive' approach to health rather than focusing on sickness and diseases.

Typically, discussions of health promotion make reference to health as a 'positive thing.' That is, conventional treatment-oriented health services are happy to stop their interventions when symptoms have been dealt with, whereas health promoters feel there is more to one's health life than the absence of overt symptoms.

(Raeburn and Rootman, 1998: 8)

The 'positive health' concept was given an initial boost by the WHO definition of health that was referred to earlier. Raeburn and Rootman (1998: 8–9) noted that "by broadening the definition beyond the absence of disease, 'anything goes' in the name of health." They defined health promotion as being concerned with positive health and well-being. The whole health-promotion enterprise is centered in a movement toward healthiness and wellness. Specifically, health promotion emphasizes that health is a matter of 'positive choice,' where individuals can learn to become healthy by altering behaviors. "The core of 'positive health' is that it is something more than the absence of disease and encompasses aspects such as "'wellness' and 'vigour and stamina'" (Korp, 2008: 24). In suggesting a theory of "healthy leadership" for corporations and other work organizations, Quick *et al.* (2007: 191) argued that "in line with positive psychology and positive organizational behavior, we consider health and the attributes of healthy individuals and healthy organizations in a more proactive way," by "breaking out of the traditional medical model."

A key mechanism of 'achieving better health' in the health promotion literature is learning, resulting in altered behaviors and attitudes. Therefore, such issues as 'perception,' 'skills,' 'competence,' 'attribution,' 'cognition,' 'beliefs,' 'motivation' and so on are critical concepts in the health promotion literature (e.g. Downie *et al.*, 1996; Koelen and van den Ban, 2004). Overall, the literature has a distinctly 'psychological flavor,' often referring to such mechanisms as 'communication,' 'symbols and meanings' and 'encoding and decoding' as being central practices of health promotion. This is not surprising given the frequent references to individuals' 'lifestyles' as the key factor of health in the health promotion literature. People's activities, behaviors, choices and attitudes are claimed to be key, where people should be motivated to run for 'healthy alternatives.' The social-psychological aspects of health promotion concern in this regard the social dimensions of health promotion through such concepts as 'values,' 'identity' and 'self-concept.' Peterson and Stunkard (1989: 822) argued that the psychological concept of 'personal control' is critical to understand health promotion's potential as a mechanism of individual change. They claimed that "belief in one's competence is closely tied to the physical wellbeing, while a belief that one is helpless is associated with mortality and morbidity." Arguing that "the link between personal control and health is well-established," they stressed that "people with high personal control are more likely to have a healthy lifestyle" and that "they avoid life crises to a greater degree than those with low personal control."

Drawing on the psychologist Albert Bandura's notion of self-efficacy (Bandura, 1997), a number of students of health promotion have argued that people with high degrees of self-efficacy, i.e. a high degree of control and management of one's life, tend to be more healthy than others (see, e.g. O'Leary, 1985; Strecher *et al.*, 1986). It is said that 'health behaviors' such as non-smoking, physical exercise, safe sex, dental hygiene, etc. are dependent on one's level of perceived self-efficacy. Arguing that "many of today's health problems can only be solved by shifting control over health practices from the medical profession to the individual," O'Leary (1985: 438) claimed that the mechanisms of self-efficacy can be an effective means through which people learn to better exercise influence over their own motivation and behavior. According to this view, "the fundamental hypothesis of health promotion is that *modification* of behavior to better fit practices associated with health and longevity will in fact increase health and longevity" (Peterson and Stunkard, 1989: 822). Lupton (1995: 56) noted in this regard that "health behaviors are mediators of health status, that health behaviors are the results of knowledge, beliefs and attitudes, and that specific behaviors, when changed, improve health." Therefore, 'knowledge' is a term frequently used in the health promotion literature; it underlies perceptions of risk and the understanding that something is potentially dangerous. Education is seen as key to behavioral change: "if people are informed about the dangers of indulging in certain activities, it is argued that they will then rationally use this information to weigh up the risk to themselves and act accordingly" (ibid.). Assumedly, the individual is a rational actor, where any lack of knowledge is seen as a source of risk.

This view on health "means that people recognize that ill health is not inevitable and that they can shape their own lives and the lives of their families free from the avoidable burdens of disease" (Koelen and van den Ban, 2004: 39). Traditionally, 'health education' has been characterized by its medical approach, where the focus has been "on the reduction of both morbidity and premature death" (ibid: 30). Koelen and van den Ban (2004: 30–32) argued that previous health education tried to make people aware of negative consequences for the health of their behavior. "Strategies to improve health were based on helping people to form sound opinions and make good decisions." Individuals were seen as logical information processors, expected to act on information in a rational manner. However, "rational cognitive appeals do not seem to possess enough power to motivate the individual to change behavior" and therefore "motivation, skills, and perceived self-efficacy are obviously important conditions as well." In addition, 'health-related behavior' is learnt in an organized fashion, i.e. in a social context. "In order to implement effective health education, the focus shifted to determinants of behavior other than knowledge—such as social influence, skills and opportunities—and the possibility of changing such behavior." According to these authors, this marked an important shift in responsibility by considering health as the 'property' of individuals, thus making it "possible to assume that people can improve their health by choosing to change their lifestyle." In sum, "individuals are encouraged to change their behavior in a certain direction seen as conducive to health in the eyes of the expert." The health promoting expert's role, just like the medical practitioner, is to guide the individual "to behave in a healthier manner." In order to accomplish this, the expert needs information regarding the targeted population, e.g. about the way they lead their lives, their view on health-related topics such as smoking, and so on. The individual must be encouraged to participate, both in the stage of planning and in the stage of execution. "In this approach, the focus is on helping people to identify their own concerns and to gain the skills and confidence to act upon those concerns." Not only do people need to improve their 'health literacy' in order to effectively understand communication from the health expert, they also need to participate in designing and implementing health education programs.

Overall, to a large extent, health promotion is seen as a 'liberating' discourse, where individuals 'take control' over their own health and life, thereby realizing a management ideology that is focused on the 'committed individual.' The 'participatory' approach, albeit organized by health professionals, is seen as a way to 'put the individual at the center.' It is an enterprise that seeks to "strengthening the skills and capabilities of individuals" (Koelen and van den Ban 2004: 37). To this extent, health promotion

> supposes making the *healthy* choice to be the most important. It therefore assumes that this is also how any rational person would act. The task for health promotion is then to remove obstacles, both individual and social structural, to this choice.
>
> (Thorogood, 1992: 73)

Similarly Downie *et al.* stressed that

> the establishment of attitudes which are conducive to health is one of the objectives of health promotion ... It is therefore of central importance to consider what attitudes are and how they can be changed. The relationship between attitudes and behavior, and situational influences on this relationship, are of particular interest.
>
> (1996: 119)

It is assumed that by *choosing* health, one makes a *positive* choice, embarking on a road that is likely to conduce or to enhance health. "To see health in this way is to see it in utilitarian terms. If a society is going to flourish then its members must be healthy" (Downie *et al.*, 1996: 173). According to this view, "health and health promotion can probably be best seen primarily as values enterprises, with the people working in these areas believing that what they are trying to do is 'good' and valuable" (Raeburn and Rootman, 1998: 8). This view was further emphasized by Downie *et al.* (1996: 2–3) who argued that health promotion cannot be seen as a way of cutting costs only: "We conclude that health promotion is justifiable on its aims alone, rather than depending on economic arguments." According to the authors, health promotion deals with values and attitudes that aim to bring about behavioral changes that are hard to evaluate in terms of costs and investments. Tones and Green (2004: 1) maintained that "health and health promotion are socially constructed. Explanations of health promotion and preferences for particular strategies and methods are, ultimately, ideologically determined." Not surprisingly then, it is widely acknowledged that health promotion is hard to evaluate in objective terms. Thorogood and Coombes (2004: 5) noted that health promotion has become a 'success story' despite the fact that systematic evidence of its effects is largely lacking. Governments and corporations are spending huge sums on health promotion each year, but the effects are very hard to measure: "One of the difficulties facing the evaluation of any health promotion activity is deciding on what value to give to 'health'." In addition, "the range of activities involved in health promotion, and the multiple levels of operation, generate difficulties for its evaluation."

The idea of health promotion as a value enterprise—concerned with liberating people—is closely related to the notion of 'empowerment.' Weare (1992: 102–3) argued that "a key principle of health promotion activity is empowerment," i.e. the active participation of the people that constitute health promotion's target group. To this extent, "empowerment is predicated on some central principles and values, most notably democracy, equity and sustainability." According to Green *et al.* (2000: 8), 'empowerment' represents a primary criterion for identifying health promotion initiatives: "An initiative can be classified as a health promotion initiative if it involves the process of enabling or empowering individuals or communities." Thus, according to this definition 'empowering' a person promotes his or her health. Overall, the idea of 'empowerment' in health promotion discourse builds on the idea that power is taken away from (medical) experts regarding health and is given to the individual. The individual is empowered to understand what is good for him or her, and what is required to stay healthy. According to the health promotion literature, active participation in terms of self-management is strongly encouraged, as is the use of many different approaches and the entry of health promotion into all areas of social life, from the home to the school to the workplace.

> The role of health professionals is to nurture health promotion by helping people to develop personal skills to make healthy choices by providing information and education, thus enabling people to exercise more control over their own health and over their environments.
>
> (Lupton, 1995: 58)

WORKSITE HEALTH PROMOTION

In the literature, the idea of a 'settings-based approach' to health promotion is a popular one, where people at a worksite, in a neighborhood, in a city, etc. are targeted (see, e.g. Weare, 1992). "Community participation means that health promotion is carried out by people and with people," where "people actively participate in the identification of their needs, setting priorities, taking decisions, and planning strategies and implementing them in order to meet these needs" (Koelen and van den Ban, 2004: 35–36). Green *et al.* (2000: 1) stressed that "most health promotion activity is bounded in space and time within settings that provide the social structure and context for planning, implementing, and evaluating interventions." The World Health Organization, (especially its Regional Office for Europe) has been a main proponent for the 'settings approach' to health promotion," e.g. by initiating "Healthy Cities" projects. To a large extent, such initiatives have gained authority from the focus of the Ottawa Charter on "supportive environments for health" (see aforementioned).

Hanson (2007: 43) maintained that public health work has traditionally been concerned with preventing illness, but today a focus on preserving and improving health is dominating. "In this approach, we focus on the whole human being and the conditions which mould his or her life." Therefore when health promotion is to be implemented, "it needs to be linked to the different 'settings' where daily human life takes place, e.g. the workplace, the school or local society." Green *et al.* (2000: 12) claimed that the 'settings approach' should have "powerful appeal for practitioners as a concrete, practical focus insofar as settings represent a pragmatic and manageable scale at which to direct change efforts." Quoting Mullen, they said that settings are "major social structures that provide channels and mechanisms of influence for reaching defined populations." Specifically,

> settings can be conceptualized as both (a) physically bounded space-times in which people come together to perform specific tasks (usually oriented to goals other than health) and (b) arenas of sustained interaction, with preexisting structures, policies, characteristics, institutional values, and both formal and informal social sanctions on behavior.
>
> (Green *et al.*, 2000: 12)

They stressed the idea in the health promotion literature to shape settings to be more conducive to 'health.'

One of the most popular targets for health promotion remains the worksite; hence, the relevance of the notion 'worksite health promotion.' Health promotion advocates have long argued that there is a relationship between health behaviors and economic productivity. The basic idea is that people who exercise, have a balanced emotional state, don't smoke, eat a good diet, and practice other 'health-enhancing behaviors,' are absent less often and are more productive when they are at work. In Europe, a number of governmental and non-governmental organizations associated with the European Union are most active in promoting the ideas of worksite health promotion on the European scene. The Luxembourg Declaration on Workplace Health Promotion in the European Union from 1997 states that "a healthy, motivated and well-qualified workforce is fundamental to the future social and economic wellbeing of the European Union." It is specified that the following issues will characterize "the world of work" during the twenty-first century: globalization, unemployment, increasing use of information technology, changes in employment practice (e.g. short-term and part-time work), increasing importance of the service sector, downsizing, increasing number of people working in small and medium sized enterprises, and customer orientation and quality management. All these phenomena suggest, according to the declaration, that "the future success of organizations is dependent on having well-qualified, motivated and healthy employees."

In order to effectively tackle these challenges, traditional occupational health services mainly concerned with health in the workplace by reducing accidents and preventing occupational diseases are seen as insufficient. Instead, by promoting health in the workplace, "organizations will see a reduction in sickness related costs and an increase in productivity. This results from a healthier workforce with increased motivation, higher morale and improved working relationships." According to the document, worksite health promotion contributes "to a wide range of work factors which improve employees' health," such as management principles that acknowledge that employees are "a necessary success factor for the organization"; an organizational culture that includes "participation of the employees and encourage motivation and responsibility"; and a personnel policy "which actively incorporates health promotion issues." Worksite health promotion is regarded as a comprehensive program where "all staff have to be involved" and "be integrated in all important decisions and in all areas of organizations." The significance of worksite health promotion is also stressed in the Lisbon Statement on Workplace Health in Small and Medium-Sized Enterprises from 2001. There it is reported that more than 99 percent of all companies in the EU are small- and medium-sized and that they make "a major contribution to growth, competitiveness, innovation and employment." A critical idea to the Lisbon statement is that worksite health promotion is particularly important as an enabler of the creation and development of innovative enterprises: "Health and wellbeing at the workplace are essential prerequisites for increased innovative potential in SMEs while, at the same time, constituting a fundamental component of modern human resources policy and management practice." The Barcelona Declaration on Developing Good Workplace Health Practice in Europe from 2003 aimed at disseminating "good workplace health practice in Europe, and to encourage all stakeholders involved to support the implementation of the vision 'healthy employees in healthy organizations'." In this document, it is claimed that "good workplace health" is the key to public health in general:

> The world of work, and the way that working life is organized in our societies today, is a major, and perhaps the strongest, single social determinant of health. Individual health practices are shaped by our workplace cultures and values ... Workplace health is not confined within the factory walls. The workplace has major impacts on the health of families and communities.
>
> (Barcelona Declaration, 2003)

The link between economic success and a healthy workforce is stressed where "successful organizations" realize that "a healthy workforce and a healthy workplace are the foundations for sustainable economic success," particularly "in the transition to the knowledge society," where the potential of the workforce becomes critical. "It is vital, and increasingly recognized, that only healthy employees enable enterprises and our societies at large to develop innovative capacities which ensure survival within the globalized competition." As was indicated earlier, health is regarded a key driver for innovative companies. "'No innovation without health and workplace health promotion' is the basis for successful strategy for preparing European industries and other businesses to respond to the new challenges." Health promotion at workplaces is seen as a vital mechanism for Europe to "become the most innovative and dynamic region in the world" (Barcelona Declaration, 2003).

The concrete manifestation of the different declarations on worksite health promotion is the European Network for Workplace Health Promotion that was founded in 1996 and that includes members from all of the EU countries as well as Norway, Iceland and Lichtenstein. On its webpage (www.enwhp.org) the following is stated:

> Operating in a highly competitive business environment and with increasing pressure on the labour market, many employers in Europe are becoming aware that they need to implement measures to improve productivity and efficiency while at the same time enhancing the working environment and company culture. Workplace health promotion has been show to play a major role in achieving these outcomes.
>
> (European Network for Workplace Health Promotion, 1996)

In one of the organization's documents, "Healthy Employees in Healthy Organizations. For Sustainable Social and Economic, Development in Europe," it is made clear that its principal mission is to spread ideas on worksite health promotion to all member states of the EU, and to employers around the EU. This is mainly done through publications, conferences and seminars, where it is stressed that "worksite health promotion is a modern corporate strategy, which aims to prevent ill-health at the workplace." In a document entitled, "Making the Case for Workplace Health Promotion," the goal, "healthy employees in healthy organizations," can be accomplished by "convincing companies and stakeholders to integrate health promotion concepts in their policies"; specifically by proposing "arguments and justifications that show the advantages of workplace health promotion activities." The organization therefore regularly publishes case studies that suggest the benefits of workplace health promotion for those companies that have integrated these practices in their everyday activities. But it also addresses policy makers and politicians by pointing out how 'sustainable economies' and 'healthy societies' can be accomplished through worksite health promotion.

A critical idea to this organization is that worksite health promotion is something different from 'traditional' occupational health concerned with national legislation on work environment, "by including elements such as work organization, organizational and human resource management." This 'new understanding' is said to encompass both physical and mental well-being, quality of life and learning.

> Health is no longer a result but rather a process in which people, with their potential and ability to develop, are viewed as an entity and are no longer merely regarded as someone to be protected against illnesses and accidents.
>
> (European Network for Workplace Health Promotion, 1996)

Worksite health promotion is regarded as particularly important in the 'new economy' sparked by globalization and information technology that emphasizes constant change.

> Staff cuts, time pressure and new working conditions such as part-time and tele-working, the high proportion of ageing workers and the increasing importance of the service sector are creating new challenges which can only be mastered with motivated, well qualified and, above all, healthy employees.
>
> (European Network for Workplace Health Promotion, 1996)

The workplace is thought of as an important arena for learning skills and competencies that are deemed valuable in this economy, including the acquisition of knowledge, experience and motivation for people "to influence their own health and their attitudes to health, both within and outside their working environment." Drawing on research publications that are said to support the idea that worksite health promotion should not be seen as a cost, but an investment that will pay off, it is concluded that worksite health promotion "leads to a situation in which there are no losers—only winners!."

The organization offers a number of projects, for instance, "Mental Health in the World of Work," a campaign that was opened in October 2009. In a document describing this project, it is argued that "mental health is important for business" in the sense that a mentally healthy person is someone who "realizes his or her own potential, can cope with the normal stresses of life, can work productively and fruitfully, and is able to make a contribution to her or his community." In essence, "employees with good mental health will perform better in their work." The campaign's purpose is to offer employers advices and experiences on how to promote good mental health: "How should you as an employer start to address mental health issues in your workplace?"; "What activities and policies do you need to set in place?." A more comprehensive project that also was launched recently is the program "Move Europe," where it is claimed that worksite health promotion can be a trigger to employee flexibility and change, and this "greater willingness to be more flexible has a positive impact on productivity." Given the idea that innovations and the constant generation of new products is seen as a key to European competitiveness on the global scene, it is argued that health promotion is a critical mechanism to increase the motivation and commitment of employees. "Companies with healthy employees have verifiably a higher creativity and innovation potential." As it is expressed in the document "Company Health Check: An Instrument to Promote Health at the Workplace," a central part of the project is a web-based "company health check" for self-assessment, "which will challenge organizations to self-reflect on WHP [worksite health promotion] and lifestyle topics." The checklist is structured around four "health topics." The first issue is "smoking prevention" that deals with matters related to how the employer tries to encourage employees to quit smoking or refrain from beginning. The second issue is "healthy eating" and revolves around the employer's efforts to stimulate employees to eat an allegedly healthy diet both on and off the job. The third issue concerns "active living," which is about the employer's efforts to stimulate a physically active life among the employees, e.g. by supporting walking or cycling to/from work. The last issue is "stress" that revolves around the employer's willingness to prevent employees from suffering from burnout or fatigue. After filling out the health check, feedback will be sent by e-mail to the employer containing "a set of recommendations with practical advice and possible ideas to stimulate and increase workplace health promotion."

A number of non-governmental organizations in Europe are also dedicated to spreading the ideas on worksite health promotion. One of the most ambitious initiatives is "Enterprise for Health" (www.enterprise-for-health. org). Members consist of major companies from various branches and industries around Europe. The organization is to offer "best practices" on worksite health promotion and to offer "a forum for quality and innovation in the field of company health promotion." For instance, one of its most recent conferences had the theme, "Driving Business Excellence through

Corporate Culture and Health" and gathered "captains from industry and decision-makers from European enterprises." In the document "Health is the Greatest Wealth," it is emphasized that "traditional management methods tied to directives and hierarchies no longer foster the motivation, creativity, commitment and adaptability that a company needs in today's competitive global marketplace." It is argued that this organization has made significant contributions to disseminating new management principles that revolves around corporate culture and values-oriented management. "It has demonstrated how individual employability and modern corporate structures go hand in hand—how companies and their employees can set new standards on the basis of personal responsibility and subsidiarity, solidarity and goodwill." Two recently highlighted issues are "Approaching the Age of Flexibility in Good Health" and "Healthy Living and Working." The first issue concerns the call among employers for more flexible work arrangements. This is seen as part of "an innovative change process." Given the alleged potential of, e.g. flexible working hours for employers, it is acknowledged that employers must take preventive actions to maintain employees' health so that they are able to cope with the new challenges that are said to arise from these initiatives. The second issue concerns "life-style related behaviors such as diet, physical activity, tobacco use and stress." It is argued that employees' lifestyles are not merely a private issue; it should also be a major concern for employers. It is argued that promoting a specific lifestyle can contribute to good health among employees that has positive outcomes on company productivity and morale. A critical idea to creating "healthy lifestyles among employees" is to design organizational cultures that foster responsibility, activity and commitment, where health is seen as an "important part of workability and employability." By creating an "employee-oriented design and orientation of work," the employees' behavior and attitudes are focused that are seen as consistent with a new management paradigm of attending to employees' ability to manage themselves.

Following this discourse, since the 1990s onward employers have given increasing attention to the promotion of a healthy lifestyle as the key strategy to spur commitment, activity, engagement and initiative among employees (e.g. Zoller, 2003; Quick *et al.*, 2007). The popular notion of 'healthy corporation' or 'healthy organization' assumes that employees are willing to learn to become healthy by recognizing "their own values and priorities and how they want to live and work" (Diamante *et al.*, 2006: 483).

> People may be among their own worst enemies when it comes to health; that is, what we eat, whether we exercise regularly, how much we smoke or drink, and how we manage stress—to name just a few of the risk factors—have a good deal to do with whether we are likely to achieve our maximum potential life expectancy—and productivity. It stands to reason that it is in the personal best interests of the

individuals, as well as in the economic best interests of their employers, to reduce these risks.

(Sloan, *et al.*, 1987: 9)

Hanson suggested,

> health and productivity in work are linked. A sound workplace with healthy employees performs better. Health can therefore be seen as a strategic resource in the organization. The task of creating optimal conditions for health is thus a strategic issue, or at least ought to be one.
> (2007: 230)

In relation to this view, Hanson maintained that health should be seen as a "competence" in order to be "adequately productive." Therefore one's health status is "one of the key to competence and the exploitation of competence" (2007: 246).

Specifically, worksite health promotion consist of such practices as risk assessments, aerobic exercise, fitness classes, smoking cessation, nutrition and weight control, stress management, healthy back programs, cancer prevention and screening, drug and alcohol abuse reduction, and accident prevention. A number of promises of worksite health promotion are often put forward in the literature, such as cost containment, reduced absenteeism, decreased staff turnover, improved employee mental alertness, improved moral and job satisfaction, and improved productivity. In essence, health promotion consists of techniques of gathering information about employee behavior as well as programs for changing behavior according to certain norms and ideas as held by the corporation. They consist of various human resource management programs that are "*designed to change employees' behavior* in order to achieve better health and reduce the associated health risks" (Conrad, 1987: 255, emphasis added). As has already been said, compared to traditional medical health programs of prevention of sickness and disease, and rehabilitation of disorders caused by injuries at work, health promotion programs generally focus not only on employees' physical and mental bio-medical conditions relevant to their professional roles; but also on their total life situation including family and sexual relations, fitness, eating, drinking, smoking, sleeping habits and so on (see, e.g. Bunton and Macdonald, 1992; Conrad, 1987; Downie *et al.*, 1996; Seedhouse, 2004). Much in line with current management thinking on the importance of managing all aspects of one's life, well-known worksite health promotion programs stress a 'holistic' approach to individuals' attitudes and behaviors, thus aiming to overcome the limits of traditional medical services as offered by employers (Antonovsky, 1987; Conrad and Walsh, 1992; Green and Kreuter, 1999).

Thus, typically worksite health promotion not only includes an employee's bio-medical disorders such as somatic and mental problems that can be diagnosed and treated through regular medical examinations and interventions; it also concerns alleged problems and risks in the employee's social life enacted both inside and outside the worksite that may constitute important sources of uncertainty for the corporation. To this extent, health promotion can be regarded as a mechanism of taming uncertainty by controlling 'risky' behavior. "In public health and health promotion, the word 'risk' as a synonym for danger is in constant use" (Lupton, 1995: 81). Risk assessment related to lifestyle choices is undertaken by means of health risk appraisals and screening programs.

> These health risk appraisals are used to counsel individuals about prospective threats to their health which are associated with behaviors deemed to be modifiable. The objectives is to promote awareness of potential dangers courted by lifestyle choices, and then to motivate individuals to participate in health promotion and health education programs.
>
> (Lupton, 1995: 82)

In a recent review of the field, Diamante, (2006: 477–78) noted that many wellness programs at the workplace are individual counseling interventions for both work-related and personal problems, "designed to improve the physical and psychological health of a workforce." Typically, these programs are based on a counseling service offered to all employees and their immediate families. They may include "awareness briefings," "training programs" as well as other interventions "to meet the needs of the client organization." Participation in employee assistance programs may either be the result of the individual's initiative or the organization's, where "a supervisor or manager notices that a subordinate seems to be having problems."

O'Donnell (2002: xx–xxi) has proposed a number of dimensions of health that are relevant to worksite health promotion programs:

Physical health, i.e. "the physiological condition of one's body." Most health promotion programs address such issues as smoking, physical activity, alcohol, etc.; *Emotional health*, i.e. "one's mental state of being," primarily the stresses in a person's life. Worksite health promotion programs that address this issue include stress management, employee assistance programs and recreation and leisure programs; *Social health*, i.e. "a person's ability to get along with others, including family members, friends, professional colleagues, and neighbors." Worksite programs that aim to promote one's social health include "child and frail-parent care programs; support groups; peer leadership development opportunities" etc.; *Spiritual health*, i.e. one's "sense of purpose in life, the ability to give and receive love, and feeling charity and goodwill toward others." Programs might include, for instance, "life-planning workshops"; and *Intellectual health*, i.e. health "related to achievements in life," suggesting "programs to enhance self-esteem and career planning and development efforts." According to

O'Donnell (2002: xxii–xxiii), three levels of health promotion programs are critical: Level 1. *Awareness programs* are said to increase people's level of awareness or interest in health promotion, i.e. newsletters, health fairs, educational classes, health screening, interactive counseling, etc. Level 2. *Lifestyle change programs* are about "lifestyle-related' behavior change," e.g. quitting smoking, exercising, managing stress, eating more nutritious foods, etc.; and Level 3. *Supportive environments*, i.e. the creation of an organizational environment "that encourages a healthy lifestyle."

MacDonald argued that "it is now obvious that corporate organizations have a unique opportunity to exert a major, perhaps even a decisive, effect on the health of the population" and that

> large-scale organizations are fond of claiming that the most important asset they possess is their workforce, so much so that the saying 'people are our most important asset' has become one of the modern-day corporate mantras. If that is true, therefore, then all corporate organizations should be interested in the health of their employees.
>
> (1998: 143)

In a similar vein, Diamante *et al.* (2006: 461–62) argued that a "wellness-focused organization" contributes to its employees' physical, mental, spiritual and social well-being.

> Such a system provides employees with tools to solve group conflicts maturely, a culture that prevents the release of harmful psychosocial elements, and a set of management practices that in general nurtures quality and management excellence in alignment with overall business strategy and customer demand.
>
> (Diamante *et al.*, 2006: 461–62)

According to the authors,

> a workplace promoting wellness brings job satisfaction, lower absenteeism and turnover, improved job performance, lower accident rates, and reduced health care and workers' compensation costs. The most important characteristics of a health organization are an organizational climate in which employees feel valued and are able to resolve group conflicts, management practices that reward workers for quality work, a sense of equity and support, and a learning-oriented and market-savvy leadership.
>
> (Diamante *et al.*, 2006: 461–62)

According to Diamante *et al.*, it is critical that employees acquire "healthy competencies" according to the following seven caveats that can contribute to their own, their colleagues' and their organizations' efficiency and development:

1. *Self-control*, meaning that "the individual consciously monitors personal levels of stress or anxiety";
2. *Positivism and optimism*, i.e. "the individual interprets failures or the confrontation of obstacles in a manner that leads to rejuvenated effort and hope" and he or she "identifies opportunities when in crisis";
3. *Ability to form affiliations*, implying that "the individual has the desire to socialize" and "be part of a social unit, team, or organization," contributing to the fulfillment of shared objectives;
4. *Ability to be altruistic or nurturing*: "The individual has the ability to help or give for the sake of giving" and he or she is able to do something for someone else "without receiving any form of acknowledgement";
5. *Agreeableness*, i.e. "the individual is able to negotiate or accommodate for the sake of progress" and he or she is "conversational, open, and easy to speak with, regardless of the subject matter or the potential to disagree";
6. *Openness to new experiences*, meaning that "the individual is driven by curiosity and a willingness to experiment"; and
7. *Ability to be self-directed*, i.e. "the individual takes action to assess, plan, and act to make self-improvements or accomplish goals."

(Diamante et al., 2006: 461–62)

Essentially, worksite health promotion is about making employees healthy in the sense of them remaining productive, self-managing and competent. In this sense, it is an important expression of the current managerial ideology based on 'concertive control.' Concrete practices of worksite health promotion can be seen as important mechanisms for generating organizational cultures that value control over all aspects of life, commitment and dedication.

In conclusion, in this chapter we have discussed literature on health promotion and particularly workplace health promotion. The discussion suggests, first, how the principles, techniques and professions that are associated with health promotion and workplace health promotion find their historical roots in a critique of traditional medical science and medical professions. It is the restricted focus of traditional medicine on individual illness and disease and its lack of attention to the whole life situation of the individual that is criticized by the advocates of health promotion. The discussion furthermore suggests how both the practice of traditional medicine and that of health promotion can be seen as forms of managing individuals in that they both establish authoritative relations between the experts of health and the individual, and seek to manage the latter for the sake of improving his or her health and well-being. Yet, whereas traditional medicine establishes hierarchical relations between the medical professional and the individual around restricted medical issues, health promotion institutes more symmetrical, non-hierarchical relations between the health expert, including broader lifestyle issues. In this sense, the principles and techniques of workplace health promotion are linked with those of the concertive control regime that was discussed in chapter 2. Both health promotion and concertive control are based on the idea that individuals become healthier and more able if they are helped to become self-managing and if they are given opportunities to bring together the professional and private spheres of their lives. In this sense worksite health promotion can be understood as a specific form of management that aims to enact modern principles and ideas of controlling organizations.

4 Scania—SPS and the 'New Employee'

This chapter introduces the case study upon which the theoretical ideas of this book are based. In Chapter 4, we propose the current management ideology of Scania, which forms the basis of our exploration of Scania's health-promoting activities that follow in chapters 5 to 7. More specifically, the main focus of the chapter is the principles of Scania's production system and the demands that it puts on Scania's employees. We account for the two major transformations that Scania's production system has undergone during a period of 60 years and discuss how these transformations have affected the conditions of work and especially what the work requires from each Scania employee. This background to the arguments in the ensuing chapters is important not only as it shows how each production system tends to presuppose particular personal and behavioral characteristics and capabilities on the part of the Scania employees; but also as it suggests how Scania's health expertise may play a role in supporting the employees to adapt to the requirements of the current production philosophy.

Scania is an internationally leading manufacturer of heavy trucks, buses and coaches, and industrial and marine engines. It operates in some 100 countries and has 34,000 employees. Scania was founded in 1891. Since then, it has built and delivered more than 1,400,000 trucks and buses for heavy transport work. Scania is well known not only for its products, but also for its stable and long-term strategic focus. It has grown organically, based mostly on internal financing, and it has continued to develop and produce the same category of products for more than 80 years. This conservative stance has also been very successful; Scania has made a profit each year since the 1940s, and it has not laid off any regular personnel for more than seven decades. Today Scania is generally seen as a very stable and attractive employer both among blue-collar and white-collar workers and it is well known for its highly sophisticated production principles that are the result of a long chain of development over a period of 60 years that comprises a limited number of principal transformations in the technical and social organization of its production. The first important transformation took place in the early 1940s when Scania received a new chairman of the board,

Marcus Wallenberg Jr, and a new CEO, Carl-Bertel Nathorst. Both Mr Wallenberg and Mr Nathorst were trained engineers and shared the ambition to transform Scania from a craftsman-oriented medium-sized company, which operated primarily in the Swedish market into a technically as well as organizationally advanced enterprise. Until then, each worker had had considerable professional discretion; he (it was typically a man) decided on the methods to use and was in charge of his own tools and equipment. Basically, each individual assembly worker received boxes of loose unassembled items and then put together entire machines or large components single-handedly. The line between production and development had also been highly blurred. Next to their role as operators in the factory, be it in the role of assembly worker, machinist, etc., the workers also functioned as a flexible service unit and as an experimental workshop for the design department. Based on the drawings from the product design engineers, workers made parts, components and sometimes complete new machines directly from design drawings.

Given the high levels of flexibility and creative skills required to function as an assembly worker, such workers enjoyed high status on the workers' career ladder. Yet, not only assembly workers but also forge and steel plate workers, coppersmiths, saddle makers, pattern makers and other skilled workers did their jobs under similar conditions. Even machining work required great skill. Machine workers themselves were responsible for pre-production engineering and for making tools and any fixed equipment. Furthermore, machining work was allocated by distributing drawings to individual workers, who then independently made the necessary adjustments to the machines to be able to produce the components specified. Indeed, in the 1930s workers generally worked independently and gradually taught their skills to apprentices. Their working methods were highly craft-oriented and their high level of craft skills gave them considerable autonomy and power vis-à-vis the management. These workers established a a small elite of Swedish engineering industry workers and acted de facto as managers over a cadre of unskilled (younger) workers. Very few of these craft workers left Scania to work for another employer and hardly any of them were ever asked to leave the company. Also contributing to the low turnover was favorable wage growth. Hourly wages were not exceptionally high, but piecework rates, which were set in free negotiations with the master mechanics, resulted in very good flexible earnings. Put drastically, the skilled workers at Scania set their own flexible earnings, which were normally twice as high as their hourly wages. This made the Scania workers among the highest-paid workers in Sweden during the 1930s. They established something of a working-class elite and are still in 2009 widely known at Scania as the 'Scania pork chop brigade'—a name given to them because they could afford to eat pork chops every day. Control and influence as exercised by these workers over their subordinates was direct and simple, and subject to the whims and subjective viewpoints by them. The general working atmosphere was highly authoritarian and most workers, except the elite, suffered from working with repetitive, simple and sometimes even dangerous tasks.

The new CEO, Mr Nathorst, who had recently turned 30 when he came to Scania in 1940, would initiate changes that ended the era of the "pork chop brigade." At Scania's webpage, where information is given on the history of the company, this development is explained as a company that evolved from being "dominated by master mechanics into an efficient industrial enterprise" (www.scania.com downloaded on November 14, 2009). Nathorst "who considered it a challenge to systematise, simplify, trim costs and expand operations" set up a new management team consisting of a range of 12 newly recruited engineers, all of them being relatively fresh from the university and none older than the CEO's 30 years. Most of these 12 new managers would stay with Scania until they retired in the early to mid 1980s. Together, they initiated a complete reorganization of production according to Tayloristic principles. That is, they thoroughly studied all parts of the production process and carefully designed a completely new factory in which each step in the production process was formalized and broken down into small rationally assembled parts. The idea was to design a production process that, seen as a whole, was highly sophisticated and efficient, but where each separate activity, each separate step in the production process, was not only simple to carry out, but where it was also easy to see how it related to the next step in the production chain. In the Tayloristic production process that was then established the 'pork-shop-brigade' and its way of controlling production soon came to be seen by management, no longer as the lifeblood of Scania's operations, but as a major hurdle to a more modernized and efficient operations. Unless they were promoted to a foreman position, all the changes introduced by the newly appointed skilled management engineers were seen by them as a form of degradation and thus as changes that ought to be resisted. As said by a recruitment officer of Scania's human resources department who had been working at Scania for almost 40 years:

> The pork-shop-brigade no longer fitted into the new Scania that was being formed. Even though some of them found new positions within Scania, most of them either left Scania freely or were forced to leave. In 1938 they were the working class elite of Swedish industrial life; in 1945 hardly any of them remained at Scania.

Sune Carlson, a renowned Swedish management scholar (see, e.g. Carlson, 1951), reported in the early 1950s in a study on personnel relations at Scania that

> practically every time a worker talked about his job, he came back to this point, that today there is not the same demand for skill or for individual initiative as there was earlier, and most of the foremen

testified in the same direction. The workers' responsibility is not less today than it was before, it has only shifted in another direction.

(Carlson and Ernmark, 1951: 58)

A growing sense of anomie seemed to characterize the new Scania. This conclusion was further stressed by quoting the CEO Nathorst:

> The responsibility of the individual worker has changed. He must today be able to carry out the most detailed instructions, and he has to take care of machinery and materials which are much more expensive than in the old days. But he *gets* instructions, he has lost the right to plan his own work. That is one of the great problems of our time, but I am afraid that we have to pay this price for our high standard of living.
>
> (Carlson and Ernmark, 1951: 58)

Carlson and Ernmark reported critical opinions by workers at Scania on "the problem of unskilled work and time studies," presenting a number of illustrative statements by workers such as this one: "In company 'X' I could plan the work myself, and decide myself how it should be carried out. Here you just get orders about everything"(1951: 57). Eric Giertz, of the Royal Institute of Technology in Stockholm, who has written a book on Scania's history that was commissioned by the company (see Giertz, 1991: 216), describes this transformation from the perspective of the workers and concluded: "It was scary when old craftsman work disappeared ... Previously excellent jobs were given to novices at new machines." Indeed, the new Scania worker was expected to be a completely different type of individual. The recruitment officer whom we quoted earlier stressed that

> the new workers needed to be disciplined. If they were given a particular job they were expected to do this job as told. But they did not need much professional skill or competence, because the type of factory system that was introduced in the 1940s and that were gradually developed, step-by-step up until the mid 1980s, made each individual job highly controlled either by technology or by rules and regulations.

As in many other industries and corporations that operated according to the same principles, there were a lot of problems with this Tayloristic production system throughout its lifespan; workers were generally not satisfied or proud to work for Scania, there were a considerable amount of accidents each year, and many reported in sick. But, as said by a human resource manager that we met, "I guess all these problems were significantly outweighed by the cost benefits that came with this system." In the late 1980s, however, Scania was having major problems recruiting people to work in their factories. At one of Scania's assembly workshops in Sweden, short-term absenteeism was more than 25 percent. That is, one of every four workshop employees was away from work, officially because he or she was sick. In addition to that two out of three production workers quit within 12 months—employee turnover each year was between 60 and 80 percent. Another human resource manager explained that "in those days—and its only some 20 years from now—working as an operator at Scania was generally seen as a sign that you were a loser. No one really wanted to work here." The problems did not merely concern the morale and motivation of the employees at Scania, but also the bad technical quality in production. This was in part a result of low employee dissatisfaction, but it also related to the technical and social organization of production. As said by a member of the executive team:

> When I came here in the 1980s most of the original managers that had begun to develop the Tayloristic production principles in the 1940s, were either already retired or were just about to retire. That opened up a space for radical organizational changes undertaken by me, our present CEO and several other young managers. Change was badly needed because we just kept on trying to produce as many trucks as we could; the costs in production was high because of all the faults that were made; and we made so many faults because everything was broken down into so many pieces that no one really could see the big picture, especially not the workers. In addition, the working environment was so lousy that many of our workers left us within a year.

To solve these huge personnel problems, all of them relating in one way or another to the dehumanizing effects of Scania's production with important negative consequences for employee health, well-being and morale, various experiments were undertaken in the 1980s; some of which had, however, already been initiated in the 1970s (see Goldmann, 1976; Norstedt and Agurén, 1973). For instance, Scania introduced "team assembly" operations. The idea was to make employees more dedicated to their jobs and able to stay healthy by giving them a broader range of tasks. Yet, as said by one manager, "neither productivity nor quality improved—quite the contrary. No one was made happier by having to insert more bolts than before." Supervisors also ran campaigns. They launched quality campaigns, and when this became too expensive, they launched cost campaigns. The manager continued: "It was campaign-based leadership without a long-term perspective. And the problems persisted." In the early 1990s, when Scania had exhausted traditional production and management methods, it sent a team to the Toyota car company in Japan to study what was behind that company's high productivity and low absenteeism. Scania engineers returned with important new knowledge that they had not been able to glean from the literature on Japanese car production methods. As it turned out, the success of the Japanese appeared primarily to be a matter of management and people rather than automation and industrial robots. Toyota's leadership system was based on a few clear basic values shared by all employees. The company also worked with a set of principles that all employees knew and understood. A senior manager said that "it was here that the first steps towards a new production philosophy were taken," which eventually became known as the Scania Production System (SPS). He continued, "the ideas underlying the SPS are relatively simple: all the things we do at Scania and every person that works here should be grounded in specific values that define Scania as a company."

Indeed, Scania's current 'organization culture' boils down to SPS which is seen as "the concrete manifestation of our core values," as one manager put it. In the internal document "Scania Production System" that describes the core ideas of the SPS, the CEO of Scania stated that "The SPS is our largest human resource management system. Everybody is trained in working together according to common principles and to behave in a manner that makes it pleasant to work together." In another section of the same document, it is stated that

> production is the cornerstone of Scania's activities ... Previously our leadership models focused on results. The priorities were ambiguous. Quality and productivity were beyond today's levels. Today results still matter, but we are also very conscious about *how* we work, i.e., what methods are we using and developing.

A critical idea to this system is "self-managing teams, where every individual takes responsibility to constantly improve the production process," as one shop floor supervisor explained. A factory manager explained that "personal responsibility and personal commitment is emphasized much more these days." Each member of a work team has individual goals that he or she is expected to meet. These goals are set in meetings with the team, where a supervisor who typically is in charge of five teams, is the chair. Evaluation of individual and team performance is done once a week in relation to "improvement meetings." According to the SPS system, each work task is 'owned' by the employee, stressing his or her personal responsibility for it. One supervisor claimed that

> there has been much 'taking care of' in this company, and we still want to be a responsible employer. But today we also talk about personal responsibility, that you always have a choice. In most cases you can chose to become a high-performing employee. This company wants to have employees that take responsibility for their job.

In this regard "one's motivation is a key factor," as one senior manager put it. "Motivated people tend to be active, entrepreneurial and interested in improving operations."

The SPS was formally launched some 15 years ago in order to respond to "inefficiency and low morale," as one member of Scania's top management team said. One shop floor supervisor recalled that

> when I started working here 17 years ago, everything was less organized and structured. With the implementation of the SPS everything has become more organized and formalized. Now, everything we do is strictly regulated and controlled. For me as a manager, it's much easier to know, 'this is correct behavior, and this is not'; and this goes for the rest of the personnel as well. Before there were many individual experts, now we all work in teams.

One of his colleagues explained that

> the SPS is a system of formalization and documentation. Every job is strictly described, every movement closely regulated. By closely documenting how our employees work, we learn about them and can help them improve by detecting deviances, i.e., behavior that departs from enacted standards.

A manager at the "SPS Office" at Scania, which is a unit that "should further develop the basic principles of the SPS and support all units in this enterprise," said that

> SPS has created a reliable and stable organization, which is key to any successful industrial activity. This is done through a system of analysis and documentation of how our employees work in order to create standards according to which everyone should work.

He explained that much of the ideas of the SPS come from the Toyota Production System that emphasizes extensive standardization of work processes "in order to detect deviances that should be corrected." A 'deviance' is something that departs from a norm. The manager said that

> this may include everything from some very technical issue related to how our industrial robots behave, to sick-listing of personnel. If an employee is out of work more than five times each year, then we regard this as a deviance that we need to address. It is not normal behavior.

According to the document that was referred to earlier, the SPS is about three fundamental aspects: (a) Values; (b) Principles; and (c) Leadership and Employee Career. Values are said to be the pillars of SPS in that "they mirror the culture of the company and what we have agreed to accept," namely *Customer first*; *Respect for the individual*; and *Elimination of wastefulness*. It is explained that "the customer" (be it an internal or external one) should always be "the focus of our work and decision making." Respect for the individual is about "the feeling of being respected by supervisors and colleagues and that we are given the opportunity to influence the operations." Elimination of wastefulness is defined as "the elimination of waste, e.g. quality problems, disturbances of the process and unnecessary work." It is stressed that "we need to make any wasteful behavior transparent."

The second aspect of SPS, "Principles," are "what guide us in our decision making and that help us reaching a stable and reliable productivity system." The principles "guide us in how to *think*. Based on that, we chose a method, i.e. how we should *do* things." A number of principles are central, the three most important being (a) *Normal activity—Standardized work behavior*; (b) *Correct individual behavior*; and (c) *Constant improvements*. The first issue, "Normal Activity—Standardized Work Behavior" is described as a constant need to reach "normal activity, where we can detect deviances." It is said that "we are in a normal activity when we operate according to the principles of SPS, i.e., we work in a standardized way ... A standardized work behavior allows us to detect deviances and to take corrective actions." A critical aspect of this is the "strict organization of the workplace" by (a) disposing of what is not needed; (b) the procurement of what is needed; and (c) systematization of the workplace. It is claimed that

> standardization is not only about *what* we do, but also about *how* work tasks are being carried out. To standardize manual labour means that it is formalized and that it is carried out in the same way each time, so that any returning problems can be detected and avoided.

The second issue, "Correct Individual Behavior," is about "making things correctly ... we have knowledge, methods and tools that help us behaving correctly. If you have behaved according to an official standard, and things still go wrong, then it is our mutual responsibility to swiftly improve the standard." Further, it is stressed that

> deviant behaviors are sources of wastefulness that we always try to dispose of. At the same time, deviances are a great source of improvement. Without them we would not know what to improve. We learn from deviances and are vigilant about them not repeating themselves. Working on correcting deviant behaviors should occur early on in a deviant process, before the problems start growing and become too large.

One of the employees said that "a good work behavior is to check on each other's work processes during construction. It can be harder to see for yourself if you're doing it the wrong way." As already implied, making 'wasteful behavior' transparent is a key idea of the SPS and it is suggested that each individual employee should start by analyzing him or herself: "Am I doing things correctly? In the correct order? With the best possible result?." It is stressed that "waste is a threat against our profitability."

One shop floor manager said that

> the SPS is about working in a correct way and making this transparent to everyone. In general, quality problems arise when people deviate from a standard by doing things their own way. Our CEO has said that 'we should love deviances,' meaning that all incorrect behavior should be made transparent so that it can be corrected.

These 'corrections' are done in the "improvement groups" that meet once a week and where all detected deviances in the production are discussed. Groups also meet on a regular basis, known as "Daily Control," in order to correct smaller deviances that have been detected. One senior manager explained that

> the SPS is about individual responsibility. As an employee, I should follow rules and routines; if not I should be held accountable. The SPS makes it possible for us to see who acts normally, and who don't, i.e., who follow our rules and who don't. As a human resource management system, it's a great source of knowledge since it helps us develop our personnel to behave correctly so that efficiency in production can be maintained.

Another manager stressed that "standardized behavior is key to any industrial production if efficiency, quality and not least security are to be maintained. These principles are to be executed by individual people." At the SPS Office, one of the employees maintained that "a culture of deviance makes it obvious who needs to work on himself in order to meet our standards" and a colleague of his said, "the whole point about the SPS is finding deviances. We try to tighten the string all the time in order to create situations where deviances occur."

The last issue of the second principle, "Constant Improvements," is closely related to the previously mentioned ideas on correct individual behavior and the work on findings deviances. Constant improvements are defined as activities that "challenge and improve" any standard operating procedure. A guiding star is the idea that "we should not work harder, but smarter." One of the employees who was interviewed in the SPS document stressed that "constant improvements are about participation and personal development. It is an exciting and positive part of the job, everybody takes part and helps each other." A colleague of hers said in the same document that "the introduction of the SPS has made our job more interesting. Everybody is involved in constant improvements, both regarding the organization of work and the product." The process of individually and collectively detecting deviances in the daily work situations, and in the improvement groups is described as "empowerment," where the employees "can influence their work." One supervisor stressed that

> it is in the work teams that deviances are detected, in this way my employees set the standards of their own behavior. It can be a tough game; you know it makes obvious who does not make it. This helps me as their boss to improve the work of the team, and in the end the production.

Finally, the last principle, "Leadership and Employee Career" concerns the relation between managers and employees. It is stressed that managers must work on "detecting deviances," which are seen as "sources of knowledge that can generate improvements." As a result, "leadership at Scania is about encouraging everyone to find problems."

Overall, the SPS is said to be an important tool for any manager to create an efficient and productive unit, where employees are motivated and happy with their work. One of the members of the top management team responsible for all production at Scania, concluded the document that describes the SPS by saying that "since the introduction of the SPS, the number of people on sick-leave has reduced substantially and productivity has gone up steadily." SPS is a system that makes it possible to enact certain behavioral standards that are seen as critical to the production, and to detect any deviant behavior in relation to these standards. The reason as to why sick-listing, which according to the methodology of the SPS is a source of deviance, has been reduced and productivity has gone up, "is probably the effective focusing of attention on these issues," as one of Scania's company doctors suggested. One shop floor supervisor explained that

> if a person doesn't perform well, eventually I will contact our health services in order to take appropriate actions. The current system allows you to detect who are potentially sick or unhealthy through data on who are not meeting expectations. That's great since then we can take proactive measures through our health organization.

Overall, the introduction of the SPS has created "a much more transparent organization, where everybody's performance is brought out in relief," as one shop floor supervisor said. "In the old days things weren't that formalized and the requirements on each person to perform weren't that explicit."

On the very basic level, there is nothing spectacular about these values: 'putting the customer first, 'respecting individuals' and 'eliminating waste' are probably values that most companies today would recognize as characteristic of their operations. "More interesting," said one manager, "are the principles we derive from those values, i.e., "Normal activity—Standardized work behavior"; Correct individual behavior—right from me"; and "Constant improvements." An SPS specialist explained that

> the third principle, constant improvements, relates directly to the first principle, normal activity, in that we should constantly try to improve everything that we do, but all the improvements that we make should also be standardized and documented. In this way, by seeking constant improvements and by setting standards, or put differently, by setting norms of performance, it becomes possible to see when someone is doing something wrong, i.e., when someone fails to achieve the second principle, correct individual behavior and thereby does not perform in accordance with our performance standards.

Hence, as already suggested SPS establishes a work environment that strives to make everything explicit and transparent. A transmission assembly worker said that "here at Scania nothing is brushed underneath the carpet and no one is able to hide. All the faults we make and everything that is handled inefficiently will eventually be revealed." In this respect, the SPS was referred to by one employee as "an unforgiving system" where all the faults that are made are revealed and where nothing is changed unless it can be shown to be an improvement of Scania's standards. A supervisor in one of the factory units explained that

> if something is changed it must be documented, i.e., established as a standard on a higher level of performance; and this higher level of standardized performance should provoke people into doing things incorrectly so that a new search for ways of doing things better must start again.

Hence,

> we should always try to raise our performance norms so that incorrect behavior and faults start to appear. Because it is first then that it becomes clear to us where the faults are made, by whom and thus, what we have to improve, and who needs to improve.

Since SPS is based on constant improvements and a constant search for ways of minimizing waste, it can be seen as an example of a 'lean production system.' Yet, a machine operator explained that

> here at Scania 'lean' does not mean that we have to work a little bit too hard, a little bit more because there is too little time and too few employees. On the contrary, the ambition to reduce waste and being lean actually means that we are formally organized to have more time and more people than we require for handling operations on a day-to-day basis.

Every employee at Scania has two formal roles that he or she is expected to play. On the one hand, each employee is given a role that is directly associated with the job the person has been employed to do, be it as an operator, financial expert, accountant, etc. On the other hand, each employee is also given a role as an observer seeking to improve a particular aspect of the organization in which he or she is part. A transmission assembly worker said that "I am responsible for quality improvements and a colleague of mine is responsible for health hazards in production. There are nine of those 'additional roles' and we are all responsible for at least one." All activities are also organized in teams which have a joint responsibility for a specific subset of activities. In a similar way the teams have dual responsibilities, handling activities on a day-to-day basis and improving the standard procedures for handling the activities. The transmission assembly worker continued, "all the teams are formally organized so that a certain amount of time is dedicated each week to deviance issues, that is, to activities where individuals tend to fail to meet our norms of performance." As already stated, each member of a work team has individual goals that he or she is expected to meet. These goals are set in meetings with the team, where a supervisor who typically is in charge of five teams, is the chair. A line manager stressed that "it's about personal and collective responsibility. Each individual has his own goals, but he depends on the group to accomplish them. This triggers everyone to support one another. It's in your own interest that your colleagues perform well too." One of the machine operators said that "good work behavior is to check on each other's work processes. It can be harder to see for yourself if you're doing something wrong." Another machine operator said that

> we're all part of strong teams and you don't want to lag behind. You want to contribute to the team, you know, many of my colleagues are my friends, you don't want to make them disappointed. So there is a combination of individual responsibility and mutual dependencies.

One of the main problems in trying to make the SPS work efficiently has been to find 'good employees' and, when needed, to help employees adapt to the SPS. As said by a senior manager:

> If you study the SPS carefully you will soon find out that it is not a very complex system, at least not if you consider its basic formal principles. By now it is so far developed that it appears almost as self-evident. I mean to continuously set standards, constantly trying to improve them, etc., no longer seem very radical or new. What is complex and problematic, however, is to embed in the organization and in the individual employees the correct mindset, the mindset that makes them work in this way.

An SPS specialist explained that

> in the 1980s we had held on to a particular system and culture of production for about 40 years. It was a system that reflected the characteristics of the typical factory worker of the time; a person with little education that required specific regulations and direct orders to be able to do things in a correct way.

A senior manager complemented this view: "In the late 1980s and early 1990s we found that many of our workers were not fit for the type of work that the SPS gave rise to." Even though the Scania employees and the union representatives had been critical toward the old Tayloristic regime because of the poor working conditions it resulted in with concomitant negative effects on people's health and well-being, they were, however, not particularly keen on the early attempts at introducing the SPS either. On the one hand, the SPS emerged as a threat to the individual employee that potentially felt unable to meet the competence requirements of the SPS. On the other hand, the employees and their union reprensentatives were also distrustful toward Scania's management. A line manager in one of Scania's assembly units recalled that

> on the one hand, the unions had always complained about the lack of autonomy and individual development that came with the old system. Yet, when SPS was introduced and gave workers precisely that, the workers and their union representatives were neither willing nor capable of embracing it as an opportunity.

This initial resistance did not only have to do with the lack of abilities of the existing workers to adapt to the new regime of production. It was also related to how the SPS was initially configured and presented by Scania's management. The senior manager said:

> In the early versions of the SPS we perhaps did not consider the employees' and the unions' interests and viewpoints enough. We had had considerable technical and economic problems that related to the old Tayloristic production regime and we needed to make Scania's production more efficient. The SPS was first and foremost a means to that end. But the union and the employees thought about this differently; they were more concerned about the content and the terms of their work.

One of the managers of Scania's Health Organization commented on this issue. He said that

> the process of developing the SPS and getting it accepted was very drawn out and complicated. Whereas the unions wanted 'good work,'

i.e., forms of work which were more stimulating and developing to the workers, without much regard for the economic consequences of changing the organization in that direction, top management wanted 'efficient work.' The present SPS was in a way what came out of this battle; a form of synthesis or compromise, if you will, in which the idea was to make a more stimulating way of working an instrumental part of a more efficient work organization.

Yet, it all presupposed that workers were able and willing to subordinate themselves, not only to a new way of organization and mode of working, but also to a new way of relating to their colleagues and to themselves. An SPS specialist said that

> previously working in the factory was an individual thing, a thing between you and the machine you operated. With the SPS, work became a matter of doing things together in teams. This required social and communicational skills that many of the workers did not have.

Furthermore, it presupposed that "workers continuously thought about how they carried out their work with the intention of trying to improve joint work processes." In addition, this active and mindful stance that SPS required from the workers also presupposed that each individual worker was keen on trying to develop and manage him- or herself as persons through the work they handled. Many of the workers did not meet these criteria. In fact, as said by one senior manager, "the majority of our existing workers were neither used to nor capable of working in this way. They were factory workers, and factory workers did not think or act in those terms."

Utimately, the SPS centers the attention on individual performance and in this regard the health, well-being and lifestyle of each employee becomes an interesting factor. One supervisor explained:

> First of all, you need to be in good shape to manage the job, both physically and mentally. It's hard work, but it's also complex and there is a constant pressure on you to improve the way you are managing your job.

Another supervisor claimed that

> people who pursue a healthy lifestyle tend to be more active at the workplace and can therefore cope with SPS better. They suggest more improvements and are more creative. From experience I know that people who don't feel well, tend to resist changes. This becomes a problem when you work according to principles of constant improvement.

Most supervisors and managers seem to believe that there is a positive link between 'a healthy lifestyle' and economic performance among the employees. One senior manager said: "Well, it's obvious, if you don't feel well, then you don't perform well, and performance is key to our production philosophy." This is also emphasized in documents and at websites. On one of these (http://career.scania.com), the following is said:

> At Scania, we are constantly developing our products, our activities and our organization. A task which involves everyone, which they can influence and continuously improve. Our working climate provides freedom for development and a strong sense of cohesion, which reflects our values and contributes to a healthy working environment. A health-oriented management and team are essential for a successful company. So we offer opportunities for you to reinforce an active lifestyle and increase your well-being. At Scania, we put a priority on your health and healthy activities which also involve the family. We want Scania employees throughout the world to feel good.
>
> (www.scania.com downloaded on December 10, 2009)

Indeed, since the inauguration of the SPS absence due to sickness has dropped significantly and is now on average two to three percent for the employees working in the facilities in Sweden. In all, SPS is about managing yourself, which is argued to have positive effects on people's health and well-being in the sense of empowerment. Seen as an expression of a 'positive' kind of management, it draws on a self-managing mode of control. In the following three chapters, we will explore how the WHP that is exercised by its health professionals at Scania is an important mechanism to accomplish this management regime.

5   Policies and Ambitions in Managing Health

Scania's health promoting activities are offered through the Health and Work Environment unit. For the sake of simplicity, this unit is henceforth referred to as Scania's Health Organization (HO). In this chapter we suggest how, in relation to the general development of Scania, the HO began to evolve and grow into a significant corporate resource of Scania. The strategic importance of the HO relates to the wealth of knowledge it accumulates about Scania's employees and the company's activities, which is undertaken through the daily activities of the health professionals who are employed by the HO. Progressively, the HO has grown larger, changing its strategic orientation from more traditional occupational health services geared toward cure and rehabilitation of illnesses or injuries, to health promotion, focusing on empowering people to adopt a 'healthy lifestyle' that is aligned with the principles of SPS.

The HO's manager reports to the Vice President of Human Relations, as well as to the "Health Council" that is chaired by the CEO of Scania. According to the manager of the HO,

> the strong support by our CEO for what we do around here is crucial to our legitimacy in the organization. When he started in the company many years ago, well before he became CEO, he was a typical technician and was primarily interested in production and engineering matters. But today he is also focused on our employees' well-being, health and lifestyle as crucial elements to the company's ability to perform and act according to the principles of the SPS. He's a humanist today, not only an engineer. Of course, the company has also changed; we all understand that the behavior and attitudes of our employees are critical. We cannot focus on engineering matters only; we also need to look at how this production is achieved by the employees.

Indeed, Scania's CEO often emphasizes in internal communication the importance of a "healthy workforce," which is also something he has stressed on numerous occasions at public seminars and conferences, in newspaper articles, and so on. The manager of HO said that being healthy is something that we talk about on a daily basis; it has become a core value here at Scania, a central aspect of our culture. In this enterprise, our CEO is a central ambassador. He understood early on the importance of thinking about health as a strategic issue, as part of the core values.

The HO unit is located in a single building with easy access for all Scania's personnel. One part of the building consists of a primary care unit that offers regular medical services to the employees as well as to their dependents (spouses and children). According to a contract with the local authorities in the city of Södertälje (where, as said earlier, most of Scania's production in Sweden is located), this unit has the same competence as any other primary care unit, public or private. Employees of Scania can come to the unit on short notice with most medical problems as long as they do not require acute care. At the unit, there is also a dental service with complete competence in most matters. This part of the building has a distinct medical character. When entering it, there is a waiting room and a desk with staff that register your arrival. Each room offers the possibility for medical examinations. Nurses are dressed in t-shirts with Scania's logo and the text "nurse" on it; doctors have private uniforms. The other part of the building consists of two larger office spaces that are divided into a number of smaller conference rooms and one large conference room. Each employee, including the members of the management team of HO, has a desk in one of the two office areas. The small conference rooms are used regularly for meetings between groups of staff. In this part of the building, there are no signs of any medical activity, and it is not open to visits by Scania employees, unless you have an appointment. Typically, staff working in this part of the building only meet Scania employees when they visit various Scania production facilities.

In the public part of the building, i.e. the medical unit, there are brochures available on Scania's health-promoting activities, as well as a document named "Scania's Health Journey," which is a historical account of the HO unit. In the other closed part of the building, there are copies of newspaper articles that stress the importance for companies to work with health promotion and the economic and cultural benefits of this enterprise. There is also information on what is going on at the unit that is of an internal character, such as activities by particular groups at various facilities at Scania, as well as statistics on sick leave reported by the plant managers of Scania. In each room, as well as on the walls of the corridors, in the entrance of the medical unit, and so on, there are posters with "Scania's health policy." This poster consists of three columns. The first column is colored red, symbolizing activities that aim to help employees recover from poor health due to sickness or accidents. The second column is yellow. This refers to activities that aim to prevent sickness and poor health. The third column is green, meaning the promotion of healthy and able behavior. From the red column to the green column there is an arrow, illustrating that the work by the HO should emphasize promoting healthy behavior rather than helping employees recover from poor health. "Essentially, we do not want to work with sick employees, we want all our employees to remain healthy," as the manager of HO said.

> This may be illusory, of course, people become sick and there will always be accidents in production. But we can minimize bad health by helping people to become healthy. This is our primary mission. Healthy employees are productive employees.

One of the members of the management team stressed that

> with our growing focus on health promotion, which is closely related to productivity and culture of the organization, we have gained a strategic position. As we gather a lot of information on our employees, their medical status, well-being and lifestyle in order to be able to promote their health, we have become a central knowledge unit of Scania. By way of our expertise, we can help managers make SPS more effective, both by helping them detect deviances in terms of incorrect employee behavior, e.g. related to ergonomics, lifestyle, stress and so on; and by helping them correct these behaviors.

One company doctor said that

> health has become an integrated part of the company's culture and philosophy. We must be operative and have a primary care unit offering traditional medical services to our employees and their families. But we must also go beyond a narrow medical focus on health by including a 'health-thinking' in the company at large. Healthy behavior creates the framework for efficient production.

One of the members of the management team of the HO unit emphasized that

> our growing emphasis on health promotion is just right. In the future, I believe we won't have our own primary care department that treats sick employees, they will have to turn to the local hospital. We will be focused only on promoting healthy behavior among our employees.

According to the manager of the HO, it is within the green category that the HO's future lies: "As long as we merely work with curing ill-health and treating accidents we will never be strategic and we will never be able to really influence general managerial issues within Scania." A health promotion specialist made a similar comment:

Even though we must of course take care of those who become ill and injured, it is our ambition not to work with sick people but with healthy people. I mean, if we can influence the employees' lifestyles and behaviors so that they remain healthy or become even healthier, then we do not have to treat those who are ill any longer. That is our basic mission, to promote healthy behavior among the employees, to move from the red and yellow categories in the direction of the green category.

Indeed, Scania's health unit has identified the SPS as its main target of interest. The manager of the HO unit stressed that "we have the ability to address how Scania's fundamental values affect our employees. By promoting healthy lifestyles, we are promoting a type of behavior that contributes to our production." A colleague of his stressed that

> this company takes care of its employees, we think about the broader picture by including all aspects of an employee's life, and even his family. These dimensions are core to any health promotion activity, so they go along very well.

A company doctor at the HO unit explained: "Essentially, 'health' is about values and attitudes." One plant manager stressed that "a central idea of Scania's image is that the company cares, and here the HO unit is critical. The medical part is not that significant since most of our employees are seldom ill." To this 'caring' dimension can be added the focus on personal responsibility of the SPS system, where each individual is expected to observe potential or already existing errors and problems and take preventive or corrective action. One of the managers of the HO stressed that "the work carried out at the HO unit stresses each employee's responsibility for staying well, thus being able to act 'normally' according to the standardized principles of the SPS." In this way "health promotion at Scania helps people to deliver, to be committed, to cope and to collaborate by making them strong and active." Responsibility for each person's success in the SPS system, i.e. ultimately his or her employability, lies with him or herself; the HO unit offers services to the employees that should promote this idea.

As will be reported later, Scania's company nurses, behavioral experts, health promotion experts and other 'health professionals' are not only seen as vital to the company in a traditional medical and clinical sense that involves the management of employees' individual health problems; but also as essential actors to maintain and further develop the SPS by acting as a kind of specialized human resource management unit concerned with the detection and correction of behavioral deviances among the employees. One manager explained:

> When I started here some 20 years ago, corporate health services were relatively insignificant. They were at hand to help those who got ill.

Today, this unit has a central and strategic position and they address all employees, irrespective of their health status, irrespective of whether or not they are sick or not. Their focus is all our employees, all the time and not only a small group of chronically or temporarily ill. It's not only about medical work; primarily it's about influencing the hearts and minds of our people, how they work and how they live.

One of Scania's ergonomists stressed that

our health services, from simple vaccination to complex psychological therapies, need to link up to a policy, a vision, a set of values. You can't just treat our employees as patients without thinking about the broader picture, i.e., Scania's production. The health policy of our unit must be based on our values, i.e., SPS. When you keep that in the back of your head, it's easier for us to work on people's health since we have a common frame of reference and a common language with the rest of the organization. We are not coming 'from the outside,' but share the values of all the other parts of the company. Ultimately, the health work at Scania is part of the idea of 'continued improvements' of the Scania Production System.

Indeed, it was in relation to the challenges of adapting not only the skills but also the mindset and attitudes of Scania's employees to the ideas and policies of the SPS that the HO began a process of rapid development in the mid 1990s. However, not long before, the HO had not been far from being outsourced to an external occupational health service company. When the economy took a downturn in the early 1990s, a group of consultants had been brought in to analyze and define Scania's core activities and set them apart from their non-core counterparts. The HO was placed in the non-core category. A manager at the HO unit recalled:

Being placed in the non-core category was not that nice. You felt like a second rate member of Scania and you were also afraid that this would be only the beginning; that Scania would start searching for an external partner instead of keeping this operation in-house

This, however, did not happen. Concomitant with the introduction of SPS, the HO was redefined as a "core activity" and was formally re-located to Scania's headquarters. This related to a number of issues: to the still high sickness absenteeism among Scania's operative employees; to the increased significance of seeing and treating the employee as a 'whole individual' who had to live well and feel well to be able to cope with the new SPS principles; and to the struggle between Scania's management's ambitions of raising the production efficiency and the union's ambitions of improving the conditions of work in production. As said by an ergonomist at the HO:

During this time I think the HO emerged as a resource that could help Scania deal with a number of problems. Sickness absenteeism was just one of them. Investing in the HO was also a way for Scania's management to show the employees and the union that the old saying, 'our employees are our greatest asset,' was not only fancy talk. In this sense I think it was a way of winning the loyalty of the employees.

Hence, before 1997 the HO was a small service unit within Scania that employed about 15 employees, who were all medically trained and worked exclusively with strictly medical issues such as work-related accidents, sickness, and so on. As already said, it was the prevention of accidents and ill health related to Scania's operations that constituted the HO's and its personnel's sole focus. During the last 12 years the HO has, however, grown substantially and it now employs nearly 100 people and collaborates with some 50 consultants. This expansion has not been motivated by a growing number of accidents and casualties in production; on the contrary, hazards and accidents have effectively been reduced during this 12-year period. Rather, it has been based in the belief that a comprehensive health organization is required to effectively address "the social challenges of working in and managing the new kind of factory regime that Scania has established," as one manager of the HO unit explained. An operations manager who had been with Scania for more than 30 years explained:

> with the SPS accidents and hazards were greatly reduced. It was the same thing with people reporting in sick—even though they were perhaps not really that sick. Even the personnel turnover began to drop significantly with the introduction of the SPS. At the same time, however, it also became obvious that good work was closely related to health in a different way than before.

So, the HO was allowed back in as a strategic, core resource. Yet, this was, as already suggested, not because Scania's pursuits of becoming a more efficient and flexible manufacturer had resulted in increased health costs in the form of sick leave, accidents and so on, but because Scania's management had become aware that it required legitimate expertise that could help make its employees ready and willing to work actively and mindfully in accordance with the new and more demanding principles of the SPS. One senior manager expressed that

> health is an integrated part of the company's development, it is of strategic importance. We must be operative and offer our employees medical services. But we must also be strategic by incorporating the notion of 'healthy employee' in our culture. Moreover, we should include the family in this enterprise since the employees' well-being is so dependent on how it functions.

Part of the fresh start of the HO unit was to install a new management team. The manager of the new HO unit was recruited from within Scania. He had been in charge of a relatively small recreation and sports department, as well as a marketing support department within Scania. The new manager had no medical background; however, he had shown great initiative and entrepreneurial skills in trying to develop the recreation and sports department into a resource that boosted Scania's employer branding, i.e. its reputation as an employer. He had also earned a reputation for being skilled when it came to establishing and managing relations with people higher up in the organizational hierarchy. According to one of his employees,

> he is very entrepreneurial and has a lot of ideas; it is due to him that this department has grown so much. He has been able to convince our CEO of the importance of focusing on employees' health and well-being in order to create a high-performing company.

His appointment as manager of the HO was, however, not uncontroversial. As said by one employee: "when he became manager, some of our physicians left us. They couldn't accept the fact that the organization would be led by a person lacking medical training. You know, some physicians are very conscious about hierarchy and so on." Those within HO who were critical typically meant that the new manager had pushed the HO away from those areas that truly constituted its core, i.e. taking care of work-related accidents and work-related rehabilitation. As said by one of the employees:

> It is within those areas that our professional expertise can really make a difference. If someone is sick or injured we can analyse and treat that. Employees who are neither sick nor injured, but eat a little bit too much, do not have enough motivation or the right lifestyle should not be our concern. Perhaps it should not be anyone's concern.

However, another employee said:

> I think those people who think in those critical terms tend to put a break on our expansion. Their view of health and health work is too narrow. Health includes more than medical screening, medication and traditional rehabilitation. It's about promoting certain behaviors in the organization, about creating a certain mindset, helping people to live and work healthier and in such a way that they also become more productive. And this is what our management team is up to, and I think that explains part of our success.

Two of the manager's deputies have a similar background in that they also lack medical training. One of them is in charge of one of the two subunits within the HO. This unit deals with strategy and policy development issues related to health at Scania. Since 2006 this has primarily involved the development and implementation of global standards of health promotion. Two of the employees of that unit are company nurses, the rest of them are work environment engineers. A significant portion of the daily work of members of this unit is dedicated to making regular visits to Scania facilities around the world for the sake of standardizing "best practices of health-promoting behavior," as one of them said. One of his colleagues explained:

> In order to develop and offer manuals, courses, training programs and so on, regarding general issues related to health and production, we do a lot of travelling and a lot of 'studying' of the different Scania facilities throughout the world. Hereby we try to develop a general knowledge base that can then be used to develop policies and principles of health promotion.

This may include creating global safety manuals regarding particular operations or the offering of global courses in "healthy leadership." Overall, the mission of this unit is to develop principles and policies which should then be implemented locally. As a way of pointing out the scope of its mission and width of the notion of health that it makes use of in its different projects, this unit's manager pointed out that many of the "principles" and "values" regarding employee behavior and attitudes that are manifested in the SPS system have been developed by this unit, e.g. standards on working hours, breaks, pace of operation, bodily movements and so on.

> In this respect our work and the philosophy of SPS are linked in a very concrete sense. We draw lessons from the production units and systematize them into standard operating procedures for all employees. We do this just as much from the standpoint of what is good for Scania as from that of what furthers the health and well-being of the employees. That is the authority that we have and the assignment that we are given.

Factory work has been the main focus of this unit, but recently it has introduced new projects which exclusively concern "healthy working standards" for white-collar employees.

The other subunit manages all the daily activities and programs within HO. This subunit is led by a person with a background as a HR manager. The unit works at a more operative level and employs nurses, doctors, ergonomists, behavioral counsellors and other health experts. Through a number of so-called multifunctional teams (see later) this subunit offers a host of concrete services at Scania's health center and at the different workplaces at Scania (see more later). The fourth member of the management team of HO differs from the other three in that she is a physician and has a more distinct and focused responsibility. She is not in charge of any organizational unit but is instead the medical specialist of Scania's leading executives, including its top management team in Sweden and higher-ranking officials abroad.

In daily work, the HO operates through a number of 'multi-professional health teams.' They make up what one of the managers of the HO unit referred to as the "structural core of the HO organization." By bringing together a large variety of individuals who belong to different professions, the teams are intended to maximize the depth and scope of the expertise that is put to use when studying and dealing with Scania's different operations. More concretely, to be able to study and deal with every potential health issue and every individual employee within Scania from as many angles as possible, each team comprises at least one of the following professional members: a physician, a medical nurse, a work environment engineer, a behavioral therapist, an ergonomist and a health promotion specialist. All in all, the HO comprises nine multifunctional teams. Each team is responsible for a limited section of Scania's operations in Södertälje, i.e. the city where most of Scania's facilities in Sweden are located. Hereby they are enabled to develop specialized experience and expertise related to the specific operations handled within this section. As said by an ergonomist in one of the teams:

> To be able to advise individuals in a way that is adapted to their specific situation at work and, at least in part, also at home, we need to have very detailed knowledge about the work procedures of each section and about its members. So we need to study those units that we work with very carefully and we need to know the people who work there; their physical constitution, if they have families, if they are divorced, etc., everything counts.

A work environment engineer in one of the teams developed this point. He said:

> one individual may have problems with his neck and shoulders because he is very tall or because he is not exercising enough or is not doing the right type of recreational exercises. On the surface another individual may seem to have the same neck and shoulder problem. The underlying problem may, however, be completely different; it may derive from stress rather than some physical or ergonomic issue, and the stress may, in turn, derive not from what happens here at Scania, but from some problems the individual has at home with his or her family. So you see, we need to know the people we work with, otherwise we would not be able to advise them sensibly.

The fact that health issues, such as neck and shoulder problems (problems which may be common among both factory workers and employees working in Scania's offices), may have completely different causes, was seen to underline the importance of staffing the teams with a range of different professionals. An ergonomist said:

> if a person is very tall and therefore tends to have problems with his neck and shoulders, then, it is a problem that I might handle. Perhaps this person needs some special equipment which compensates for his height. If, however, the same problems derive from stress and family life, then a psychologist should perhaps handle that problem.

According to several employees at the HO unit, it was because of these faculties of the multi-professional teams that they thought the HO had become one of Scania's 'strategic resources.' One of the managers of the HO said that:

> in the 1990s when it was often discussed whether the HO should be kept as an in-house resource or if it should be outsourced to an external provider, we had to show why keeping the HO in-house really brought something extra. I think that the teams have managed to do that; we have managed to prove that one of the great advantages of keeping occupational health services in-house is that you can build a substantial and detailed knowledge base about the company and its personnel that is critical to the effective functioning of SPS.

A physician in one of the teams made a similar comment. He said:

> an external occupational health service company will never be able to study the operations and the people as closely and extensively as an in-house unit such as ours can. I mean, we have access to Scania's employees and their production facilities every day and we have come to know the production lines and the people who handle them quite well. We have studied them closely and documented every hazard, every sickness, every change in production and all the health-related effects they give rise to for a very long time. The wealth of knowledge you get from that is impressive.

The teams are involved in Scania's operations in the role of experts and consultants. Even though they do have a practical responsibility for the general safety of the work environment and are held accountable for the professional diagnoses and the expert judgments they make, ultimately it is the line managers at the factory units who are formally responsible for keeping the work environment free from hazards and health risks. On the one hand, the teams are brought in when accidents do happen, when the personnel have health problems or when decisions are made that may affect the safety and risks related to the work environment—e.g. if new equipment is procured. About once a month at least one member of the teams makes routine visits at Scania's production facilities for the sake of learning whether or not something has been changed, accidents have occurred, if people feel well, need rehabilitation, etc. On the other hand, however, the teams also make suggestions to various changes which are not based on any concrete problems. A nurse said: "we do not merely react, i.e., we do not merely come in after the fact, after an accident has occurred or after a line manager has informed us about some health problem. We also take initiatives proactively." The ability to take initiatives proactively was explained to be directly related to the knowledge that the HO has accumulated about Scania's operation. This knowledge is manifested and made use of at separate levels: on a general level, in the form of a computerized knowledge base that the HO manages through statisticians that store and analyze all the data that the teams generate; on a more concrete level, in the form of specific knowledge about operative processes and people. A physician said:

> we have been able to accumulate so much knowledge about the different units that we can take initiatives and suggest various changes to how people work, changes in the equipment they use, or even changes which relate to specific groups of employees' lifestyles, without there being any acute problem that needs our immediate attention. If the personnel of one production unit show higher stress figures we can run the numbers statistically in a variety of ways to find out if there are any causal relations that we should study more closely. Based on these analyses we suggest various changes to the line managers and to the people directly involved.

Hence, critical to Scania's expansion of its health services is that it no longer only offers medical expertise such as doctors and nurses, but also offers a host of health-related competencies, e.g. therapists, behavioral experts, psychologists, work environment engineers and counsellors. This expansion is motivated by "a growing concern for people's ability to remain healthy, i.e., active, committed and motivated," as one manager said.

> Previously our activities in this area were kind of reactive. For sure, we have worked hard on improving the working environment, thereby preventing many illnesses or accidents that were common in the past. But we didn't focus much on people and their behavior, we were not active in promoting their health and well-being. Medical services were offered after-the-fact so to speak, when people were already ill or had suffered accidents. In order to promote good health, we need a more extensive spectrum of competencies that can address many aspects of people's performance.

One of his colleagues said that

> the SPS offers us a way to individualize production and in this enterprise our health services has an important role to play. Today everything is about personal responsibility. The company wants people who take responsibility and who are active in improving the production process.

By extending the range of services from traditional medical activities, to issues related to the broad and ambiguous notion of 'health,' legitimacy can be created to affect a host of issues related to self-management by Scania's employees. In the name of 'promoting health,' the HO unit can take initiative regarding the development of core principles and values as outlined by the SPS.

Nevertheless, one of the nurses said,

> the management team only talks about the green phase of our health policy, they tend to forget that all serious health-work is grounded in medical competence as is the case today. We who have medical training respond to real needs in the organization, we don't just talk about the importance for our employees to stay healthy.

One of the work environment engineers emphasized that

> in this kind of production, a safe workplace must come first, then you can start talking about people's health, their lifestyle, sleeping habits, fitness, and so on. At Scania, safe machines and equipment have always been key, we need to maintain that focus. Traditionally, we have had a physical/ technical perspective. Now this new organization tends somewhat to replace that by paying more attention to attitudes and behavior. There is a risk that we are throwing out the baby with the bathwater here. The idea that health is one's own responsibility can be a dangerous one in this kind of environment. You can't start talking lifestyle if the environment is bad.

Similar attitudes were expressed by a company nurse who argued that "classical clinical issues related to the work environment must not be obscured by modern ideas on promoting a certain behavior in the name of health." One of the managers of the HO unit said that "this new order has created frustration among some of our employees who previously dominated the organization. They are dissatisfied of not being at the centre of attention any longer." Overall, engineers, doctors, nurses and physiotherapists were of the opinion that technical and physical issues related to the work environment were critical to prevent illness, injuries or even death among the employees; while health promotion experts, psychologists and behavioral counsellors tended to emphasize employees' choices regarding lifestyle, habits and so on. The former group experienced that their 'classical' work was being degraded. One health promotion expert said:

> Doctors and nurses often lose sight of the broader picture. They get stuck in individual problems without being able to link our employees' behavior to the organization's goals and strategies. Their mindset remains reactive, it's about curing and preventing diseases; not about teaching our employees how to remain healthy.

Another health promotion expert argued that

> our management emphasizes health promotion, it's about attitudes and values. When you are a doctor you look for what is problematic. It's the same thing with the other guys, the engineers. I, on the other hand, look for what is good and works well, I focus on what is healthy behavior.

One of the nurses explained that "maybe the reason as to why our bosses tend to neglect the medical aspect of our work is that they lack competence in that area. It's easy to talk about healthy behavior; it's harder to understand complex anatomical issues." The manager of HO emphasized that "we need all competencies in our teams, both the clinicians and the others. What is important is, however, to think about health promotion rather than passively waiting for already sick patients to arrive. There is the paradigm shift." One of the engineers still thought,

> well, what counts in this organization is results. You don't see results easily from a health promotion activity such as a course in positive thinking. But you do see results when we have been out there, redesigning the physical workplace. Plant managers listen to us, they need us since we attend to real problems.

A doctor claimed that

> the focus on health promotion is good, but this message can't be communicated without us legitimizing it. This discourse must be grounded in a medical model, that's what gives it credibility. So this organization needs people like me, both to deal with physical and mental problems among our employees and to spread the message of lifestyle change.

A member of the management team of the HO appeared to be aware that some of the HO's professionals were critical of its new strategic orientation toward promoting health ('green activities') rather than treating or preventing illnesses ('yellow' and 'red' activities):

> We know that the emphasis on working in the green category has frustrated a few of those employees who belong to the professions that previously dominated the work of the HO. Environment engineers, physicians, nurses and ergonomists used to be at the centre of things; now other groups of professionals, such as health promotion experts, psychologists and therapists have become just as important.

Yet, the frustration among these groups of professionals did not merely concern the tendency that the new professionals and the new, green, types of activities had gained in significance, while traditional professions and their red and yellow activities had decreased in significance, it also concerned how the movement from red to green involved a transformation in values and objectives. A nurse said,

> the objective of the green activities is not to treat peoples' health problems; it is to influence and motivate people to adopt certain lifestyles and mindsets. I think it is somewhat questionable how far we should go in trying to change that.

The management team appeared to see this attitude among some of the traditional occupational health care professionals as problematic. A member of the management team said that

> there is a tendency among some of our staff to hold on to a restricted and strictly clinical definition of health care and occupational health care. There is obviously nothing wrong in this, but I think it makes them fail to see how they could be strategic resources within Scania by contributing to the SPS. I mean, if we only focus on ill-health and accidents and fail to appreciate how employees' attitudes and behaviors link to health and well-being, and in turn, how health and well-being link to corporate goals and procedures, we will never be more than a marginal resource within Scania.

However, some members of this group of professionals meant that it was precisely an emphasis on the green activities at the expense of the red and yellow activities that would undermine the HO's long-term abilities of establishing itself as a strategic resource. For instance, one physician said that

> at the end of the day, what counts are results. It is very difficult to show clear results based on health-promotion activities. Yet, measures which are taken to improve the physical work environment often lead to

concrete results. It is the same thing with rehabilitation activities. If we merely do 'green work' and neglect yellow and red work, it would not take long before someone upstairs start questioning the value of that which we are doing.

Another physician meant that

> I think the turn to health promotion is important both for Scania and for the HO. But to be able to come across with the message that we should help employees take care of their health so that they become both more motivated and more productive, we need to be seen as a strong, well founded and legitimate unit. Medical expertise and the skills that we have in handling the red and the yellow activities provide that foundation. Hence, my point is not that green is bad, but that an efficient handling of the red and yellow categories is what opens up legitimate possibilities of working with the green activities.

The aforementioned statements point toward how the credibility of the HO is dependent upon its ability to maintain some kind of balance between the red, yellow and green activities of the HO's health policy. As has already been implied, such a balance is also seen as critical from a moral standpoint. For instance, an environment engineer said that

> at Scania where industrial production is still a core activity for the majority of employees, a safe and sound working environment must be the first priority. There is a tendency today to replace that priority with a priority of healthy behaviors, lifestyle issues, attitudes and so on. Personally, I think that change of emphasis is dangerous; because before you start telling people that they are expected to take responsibility for keeping themselves healthy and productive you need to be sure that you, as an employer, have taken responsibility for keeping the working environment as free as possible from health risks.

A physician made a similar comment:

> To the extent we work more and more with green activities we actually ship a lot of responsibility on to the shoulders of our employees. Because even though we have a responsibility when it comes to teaching and coaching them, it is ultimately they themselves who must choose lifestyles, eating habits, and so on, that make them healthy and productive.

The last statements point toward how the policy shift from red and yellow to green also implies a partly new distribution of responsibilities that is aligned with the fundamental ideas of SPS to focus on 'self-management.' This is reflected in two sub-policies that the HO builds its operation on, namely the policy of 'employee-ship' and 'the 24 hour employee.' The notion of employee-ship is used generally within Scania and specifically within the HO to underline that the relationship between Scania and each individual employee should be understood, not merely as an exchange of services, but as a far-reaching contractual agreement. On the one hand, this agreement should underline that a Scania employee is a 'corporate citizen' with rights to demand that the work he or she carries out is safe and meaningfully adapted to his or her unique individual capabilities. One of the nurses within the HO said that

> most of the things we do here revolve around this notion of employee-ship. I mean, we should try to make the work environment as safe and sound as possible and we should see to it that the employees are as well equipped physically, mentally and technologically to be able to handle the work they have been given.

On the other hand, the agreement of employee-ship is also meant to underline that each employee is responsible for keeping him or herself in a work-able condition as part of the general principles of the SPS. As said by a human resource manager "every employee should know that we expect them to come to work in a condition that makes them ready and able to work in accordance with our jointly agreed routines and performance standards."

Scania obviously has no formal rights to interfere with what an employee does in his or her free time after or before work. Yet, as said by a line manager:

> If one of my employees does not sleep enough because he plays poker all night, it is his own business as long as it does not affect his ability to work. But if it does affect his ability to work—and most likely, it will—it is not just his own business, but my business as well.

Hence, the policy of employee-ship implies wide-ranging responsibilities both on the part of Scania and on the part of the employees. The width of those responsibilities is reflected in the other sub-policy concerning "the 24 hour employee." As stated by a HR manager, the meaning of this policy is that "Scania cares for its employees, both on and off the job. We try to help them live healthier. Our interest and care for the employees does not end when they leave work." Yet, it also means that employees are expected to 'take care' of themselves also after working hours. That is, the notion of "the 24 hour employee" indicates that that which happens during the remainder of the day also requires attention, care and management. One of the managers of the HO explained that

> those two policies make it quite clear how broad and encompassing our mission actually is. They indicate that it falls within the limits of our responsibilities to do everything we can to help Scania's employees fulfil

their obligations as employees and to help Scania to fulfil its obligation towards them. This may concern anything from making sure that the machines have no sharp edges to helping employees lose weight.

Yet, some of the HO professionals underlined that there are delicate issues implied here. A behavioral expert stressed that "whereas the employees have a direct right to demand that Scania sees to it that the work environment is safe, Scania cannot command their employees to eat properly, to exercise, and to educate themselves." Likewise, a health promotion specialist said that

> we can provide them with the necessary knowledge and skills and inform them about the responsibility they have to keep themselves in shape, but we cannot obviously demand that they actually do what we advise them and want them to do.

On the other hand, one company nurse pointed out that

> you employ people because they have certain competencies and abilities that are required to do a certain job. Even though it might not be spelled out officially this tends to imply a lot of health-related things such as physical fitness, personally traits, and so on. Those are part of the resources that an employee is expected to bring to work.

In that connection, a colleague of hers underlined that

> many of those resources, i.e., basic physical and psychological fitness, personality traits, etc., are developed and maintained after work in and through the life the employees lead; if you never read anything, just sit around watching stupid things on TV, and if you only eat fast-food and never do any exercise you might end up as a rather unattractive and useless employee.

Even though the HO has no right to command employees to live in such a way that they manage themselves in order to remain 'attractive' and 'capable' employees, the policies of "employee-ship" and "the 24 hour employee" are still meant as ways of pointing out that this is part of what Scania expects from its employees. In this respect, the fundamental meaning of the two policies is that the employees have the right to demand that they are provided with the opportunities—the necessary knowledge and skills and facilities—to live healthy and well, but it is still their own responsibility to use these opportunities so that they remain healthy, well and productive. As said by a health therapist:

> we constantly let the employees know that they have a responsibility for their general health and well-being and that this matters for their work.

We want the employees to feel group pressure, because, you know, one individual is another individuals' working environment. So, even though we say that we offer our employees this wide array of activities and programs and want them to choose them freely to improve their health and well-being, they cannot just say that they do not care about any of this. I mean, it is brought up when we recruit people and also in the yearly development talk that all employees have with their superiors.

However, when an employee is formally diagnosed as medically sick, then he or she is obliged to follow the prescriptions of Scania. As said by a physician:

> if someone is away from work because he or she has been diagnosed with a knee problem, which, at least in part, is caused by this person's overweight, it is his or her obligation to follow the diet and the exercises that we prescribe.

In general, this relates to rules about illness and injuries that are followed in most welfare societies. In Sweden, this specifically relates to a new set of rules concerning rehabilitation of sick or injured employees. These rules basically say that if the rehabilitation programs provided by the occupational health care specialists have not led to significant improvements of an employee's general ability to carry out his or her work after three months, this should be taken by the responsible medical professional as a sign that the employee is ill-equipped for his or her present work. The employee's own motivation and activity in trying to become healthy, well and able to work should also be considered as part of the diagnosis of the individual's state of health, and thus of his or her ability to continue carrying out his or her work. Limited health improvements or limited motivation and activity in trying to become healthy again can be taken as a sign that the employee is inappropriate for his or her job and should seek other assignments within Scania, or, if such assignments are not available, that the employee should end his or her employment with the company and seek a new job with another employer.

6 Spreading the Ideas and Ideals of Health Promotion

In this chapter we focus on how the programs and activities of the HO relates to Scania's main operations. Of special interest is to what extent and how the HO strives to affect employees in finding the strengths they need to adapt to the requirements of the SPS by constantly improving their health, and to what extent and how the HO tries to shape and adapt this production system to the needs and abilities of Scania's employees. This is done in a number of ways, where we concentrate on the role that the HO's medical clinic plays, and the importance of a regular presence of the HO's personnel in the production line. To gain a better understanding of how the HO manages a delicate balance between the requirements of the production system and the requirements of the personnel, we then explore how the health professionals interact and negotiate with Scania's managers who are to execute the SPS in the daily and concrete production.

As already mentioned, part of the HO unit consists of a regular medical clinic that is open to all employees and their families and that offers regular medical services. As an employee, one may sign up as a patient with another provider of these services that is not owned by Scania, but employees are strongly encouraged to choose Scania's unit. A manager said that "of course we want all our employees to go here." One employee said that "it's so convenient to have access to this unit since it is close to my working place" and another person claimed that "I feel like a VIP-person compared to my neighbours and friends who don't work for Scania. It's always easy to get an appointment and I can always bring my children there if they have a cold or so." One of the managers of the HO unit stressed that "our service level is much higher than the ones offered at other clinics and we try to convey the feeling to our employees that we are their 'family doctor,' you know, always there to help and support." Each employee visits this unit regularly as part of a compulsory medical check-up program. These visits consist of analyzing one's body mass index, blood pressure and making a physical fitness test. The data from these examinations are stored as an individual case record that can be accessed only by designated medical staff. The data is also lumped together with the data of the person's team colleagues that is then analyzed by the HO unit's statisticians.

If, for instance, "there is a deviance of the body mass index in the group," as a company doctor said, the HO unit contacts the manager of that unit in order to propose "appropriate actions to deal with these problems of poor health." In addition to making a regular medical examination, the doctor or nurse should initiate a conversation on the person's lifestyle, irrespective of the results of the medical screening. "I talk with the employees on their habits, such as diet, sleep, stress, as well as how they experience their family life," as one nurse claimed. She continued:

> For instance, we have a group of employees who work with research and development and who are highly skilled and qualified. They are very seldom or never absent due to sickness. They have good control, a healthy lifestyle, they eat good and nutritious food, they don't drink too much, rarely use tobacco, they exercise a lot. However, 'balance in life' is hard for this group, and they risk becoming burned out. By talking about 'domestic stress,' relationship problems and similar personal issues, we can help these seemingly healthy individuals to live even healthier lives. You know, it's not normal never being sick.

One of her colleagues called these conversations "motivating talks" and explained:

> The medical examinations are fairly straightforward and follow our internal routines for maintaining a safe working environment. We need to know that our personnel can handle the job, it's the same thing for flight pilots, police officers, and so on. But the talks afterward give us an opportunity to help the person do something positive for his or her current health. You can always improve your health! We have great resources here, various competencies that can be a support for an individual to live a healthier life.

One of the company doctors thought that the medical clinic is critical to the efforts of the company to promote a 'healthy lifestyle' among its employees, since

> it offers a forum for meeting each employee and talking about his or her well-being and lifestyle; it's one of the greatest gains. In addition to the data that we collect on the employees' medical status, we as professionals learn a lot about them, both regarding issues related to work and related to their private lives. In our role as a service unit to the rest of the organization, this knowledge is invaluable as it increases our sensitivity to the demands and requirements of our personnel. From both medical examinations and from conversations on employees' health we come to learn things that remain obscure to the regular Human Resources department. I guess people are much more frank and open about themselves when talking to a doctor who has professional confidentiality.

The medical check-ups are also compulsory for Scania's top management team. A doctor explained:

> This is important both symbolically, and practically. The former has to do with the importance of being good examples, the latter has to do with their insurances regarding pension and so on. The data gathered from the management team's medical screening is also collected and analysed at the group level. They too, work as a team according to the principles of the SPS and may get good advice from us on how to improve their operations.

Internal surveys at Scania suggest that the majority of the personnel finds the medical check-ups valuable as they "stress that Scania cares," as it was expressed by one employee. One of his colleagues said, "I think it's great that they have an eye on our health status and that you can get advice on how to avoid becoming sick or ill. Everyone wants to stay in shape." Another person argued that "it's not dramatic at all, you just go there and take these tests and then you have an informal conversation with a nurse." Yet one person thought that

> it's sometimes like a 'nanny corporation,' you know these questions on what you eat, how often you drink and so on. I don't think that they should be of any concern to my employer. Sure, they may affect the way I perform at work, but there must still be some privacy around here.

Another individual claimed that

> you don't have to answer all these questions, it's the medical part that is compulsory. I have said to my doctor that I don't want to talk about my exercise habits, and he thought that it was OK. Instead he gave me general advice on the importance of physical exercise, and that was good.

As part of the routines of the HO unit, the medical personnel, i.e., nurses and doctorsshould also have 'health conversations' when employees visit the medical unit on other occasions than during the compulsory check-ups. One of her colleagues said,

> I always end the examination by asking about how they feel at work and at home, if everything is fine, and I briefly tell them about our services, so that they can ask their manager to visit us if there should be a need in the future.

Also, the persons working at the unit's telephone service should have conversations related to employees' health and well-being. One of the nurses said that "when someone calls regarding high blood pressure and wants to see a doctor, then it's a good opportunity to talk about diet and exercise as well. Perhaps this individual should see one of our health promotion experts as well?" A colleague of hers said that

> the other day it was a woman who called, a relative to an employee. She was really upset since he did some strange things at home due to alcohol. You know, we're open to employees' families as well. Well, we decided to make an appointment with one of our doctors the next day so that we could form an opinion on the matter.

She recalled that this meeting was held between the personnel from the HO unit and the employee and his spouse, and that the conversation ended up in a rehabilitation program for the employee. The nurse explained that

> even if a person behaves well at work, he may hide problems that only relatives see. But these problems may become ours as well. It's much better to prevent them from happening rather than just waiting. It's a quite common situation regarding drugs and alcohol. People avoid drinking at work, but if they drink at home, this may affect their work in the end.

Another common forum of interaction between the personnel of Scania's health organization and the rest of the company is through regular examinations of machines and equipment regarding safety and ergonomics. These examinations are conducted by work environment engineers and ergonomic experts. Each workstation is closely scrutinized in order to prevent injuries, as one of these professionals explained. This means that each "work position" has been examined by an ergonomic expert regarding how the person stands, what movements he or she makes, and how he or she can use supportive advice. One ergonomic expert said that "we make a schema of appropriate movements that we call 'the healthy way.' We expect our employees to follow them and report to us if they encounter problems so that we can take corrective actions." Each work position is documented and standardized according to the philosophy of the SPS. Another ergonomic expert said that

> we try to constantly improve the way each person's work position is described and constituted in order to prevent people from becoming ill. This is how we, as ergonomic experts, contribute to the organization's health promotion, by helping people remain healthy.

These examinations are conducted together with the manager of the workstation and the employees who work there, where the latter ones can show existing movements and activities. In this way "we can help improve both the situation for each employee and for the work team who can produce more efficiently," as the ergonomic expert put it. During the examinations we pay much attention to the work that is to be carried out, for example the assemblage of heavy equipment and try to see what human movements are bad or unnecessary, and what movements should be promoted." A colleague of hers stressed that

> we can't only pay attention to the physical work environment, but we must of course look at how individuals interact with machines and equipment. Part of that analysis focuses on the behavior of the employee and his or her potential to behave in a healthy way from an ergonomic point of view.

She explained that, for instance, some obese persons have problems in following rules regarding how to lift equipment.

> We try to approach these individuals by talking with them about their lifestyle, their habits, what they eat and drink and so on. People who are not healthy may need help if our rule of how workplaces are to be designed is to be maintained.

A similar view was put forward by one of the work environment engineers who conducted examinations of machines and equipment in order to avoid accidents that may cause injuries or even death among the personnel:

> The work on a safe and sound work environment is the basis for all production in this company. Our work is much appreciated in the organization. This creates an opportunity to create long lasting and trustful relations, where we may help units to become healthier. People who are tired, who lack commitment and drive, who have poor relations at home can be dangerous to themselves and to other people. Even if we try to design machines that are safe, accidents will happen if people make mistakes. And mistakes are often made by people who pursue an unhealthy lifestyle. When we examine machines and the physical environment we should also, in collaboration with the manager of the unit, discuss how the health of the personnel may be improved.

One of his colleagues said that

> like flight pilots in this organization you are entrusted with sophisticated tasks and you often work with equipment that is very expensive. Therefore we need to ensure that our staff has the ability to perform well, both in a physical and mental way.

These practices of maintaining an atmosphere of personal responsibility and 'self-management' is particularly important during both the regular examinations of the workplaces and the examinations that are conducted when a new machine has been installed or when the workplace need to be redesigned in order to meet new production targets. As representatives of Scania's health organization that operates according to a certain 'health policy,' which aims to promote a healthy lifestyle among all of Scania's personnel, ergonomic experts and work environment engineers have an opportunity to affect how employees regard themselves concerning both mental and physical risks. One of the work environment engineers said that

> by addressing problems in the work environment such as the design of a particular work station, we also have an opportunity to address problems among our employees. The one presupposes the other if we are to maintain an effective production. Earlier work environment engineers didn't care much about people and their health and lifestyle. They were only focused on machines and equipment. But by working in teams with health promotion experts and people with similar qualifications, I believe that we have come to appreciate how important it is for the personnel to stay in shape if dangers in the workplace are to be prevented.

One ergonomic expert thought that

> constantly working in a team with other health professionals makes it possible for us to address a much wider range of issues related to both employee behavior and workplace design. Our employees are under strong pressure to perform well, and their own mental and physical constitution as well as equipment and the workplace itself is a key factor in that regard.

A manager of one of the plants was of the opinion that the regular presence of work environment engineers and ergonomic experts was not only positive from the point of view of maintaining a good and sound work environment in order to prevent injuries and accident, but that

> it also has an important symbolic value. Our work environment standards are much higher than what is requested by law, and this shows that Scania takes care of its personnel, it's part of our culture to do more than what is requested by society.

One shop floor supervisor was of the opinion that "dedicated and committed employees thrive in an organization that stresses the importance of health and safety at work." According to him, ergonomic experts and work environment engineers were "central in conveying the message that 'this organization puts the individual at the centre'" that concretely is accomplished by "empowering and supporting." One employee thought that visits by ergonomic experts and work environment engineers were part of the weekly routine, "where they talk to us about maintenance and repair, how work positions are designed, and what we can do personally to better cope with the job." One of his colleagues recalled how one of the ergonomic experts of the HO unit had video-filmed him and his teammates during one day, and returned with feedback after a week at one of the weekly "improvement meetings" that is a central routine of the SPS. At that meeting

> she [the ergonomic expert] had a lot of remarks on how we moved equipment and handled some of the apparatuses that could cause injuries and proposed a number of suggestions of improvement. She made us aware of a number of deviances. Two of us were asked to see one of their health promotion experts as it seemed to her that we had problems in coping with the current design of the workplace.

Documenting by video how people work at the workplaces is a common practice by ergonomic experts "in order to suggest how people can work smarter, not harder," as one of them said. Working 'smarter' means working in a way that "your health and ability is maintained at the same time that you perform better and better." The concept of "healthy organization" that is pursued by the HO unit links directly to the work of ergonomic experts and work environment engineers. One of the managers of the HO unit said that "the concrete work environment must be healthy, meaning that people not only become ill, but that they feel motivation, commitment and drive." One of his colleagues stressed,

> the work done by the ergonomic experts and the work environment engineers is perhaps the most important work by all our health professionals since they create the ground for interaction between us and managers, and us and the rest of the employees. Their work that is requested by law is compulsory, and is therefore an indispensable channel to promote the health philosophy of Scania.

The formal work environment is, however, not only the formal responsibility of ergonomic experts and work environment engineers. Behavioral experts and health promotion specialists are involved in regular examinations of the "psycho-social work environment," as one of them explained. One of the said that "we do regular check-ups regarding discrimination, mobbing, drugs and alcohol and related issues." Individually and during team-meetings employees are requested to inform these experts on "the psycho-social status of the group or of the larger worker place," as one health promotion expert explained. "We ask questions on how they experience the climate, the communication between each other, the way people address each other, and similar things," a behavioral expert said. These examinations are related to the issue on "respect for the individual" that is a central value of SPS, and "if we find that, for instance, there is a raw attitude among the colleagues, or discrimination due to sex or ethnic background, we report this as a 'serious deviance' that needs to be corrected promptly." The psycho-social environment is said to be "closely linked to the values of this company and is critical to maintain good health among the employees. It's about behaving in an appropriate way towards one another."

One of the managers of the HO unit reported that

> the values and principles of SPS must constantly be enforced and that is part of our job, we don't want them to remain nice paper products, we need to support the units to work according to them, where ultimately our examinations are no longer needed.

He mentioned that a "good work environment is characterized by mutual commitment and joy, no individual is excluded and everybody should feel part of our mutual work towards constant improvements." Specifically, the examinations consist of a written survey that each employee is to fill out regarding questions on conflicts between colleagues, conflicts between employees and supervisors, the ability to influence the activities at the work-place, interpersonal communication and similar issues. The results are aggregated to the group level and then discussed with the supervisor of the work unit or his or her closest manager. "If problems are seen to prevail according to the values and principles of the SPS or if a work unit does not function according to the Scania culture," as one supervisor said, then a meeting is held between the specialists from the HO unit and the manager in charge of the workplace. "We try to hold these meetings in a constructive and positive manner and emphasize that the examinations are about detecting issues that can make people sick," one of the experts said. A colleague of his stressed that "research has shown that a poor psycho-social climate reduces people's commitment and motivation as well as increases the risk for heart diseases, somatic problems as well as mental ill-health."

When problems are suggested by either the HO specialists, the employees themselves or by managers, various measures can be taken. For instance, if there is a problem of alcohol among some members in a work group, then these members are offered a rehabilitation program "to get rid of their abuse and control their future behavior towards alcohol," as one of the health promotion experts explained. This program that is offered outside Scania is paid by the company. The person must sign a contract that stipulates that if the person does not follow the program's rules, then in addition to paying for the program out of his or her own pocket, the person is fired. If a poor working climate is allegedly due to, for instance, conflicts at the workplace, then all members of a work team can be sent for a course on 'team building' that is held by the HO unit. These team-building programs that take place once a week during four months consist of both physical training such as swimming, skiing, basketball, football, dance and climbing, as well as lectures on communication, cultural awareness and respect. One behavioral expert explained that

> these courses are about creating teams that work well, where conflicts are avoided. When we behave in a trustful and respectful way toward each other, our well-being and motivation increase. Some managers may find that these programs are just rubbish, but it's all about creating good conditions for individual health and productivity. People are no robots, but must feel well and at ease.

One employee that took part in one of the team building programs said that

> I feel much better these days about going to work. We had a bad climate in the group, there were two guys that tried to dominate, but now we are all much more on an equal footing. The efforts by the personnel from the health department have been great in trying to create a team that works well. I think this affects both how you feel and how you perform, so it's a gain both for us and for the employer.

The formal responsibility for maintaining a work environment that is consistent both with national Swedish laws regarding the physical work environment, drug and alcohol abuse, discrimination and related issues, and with SPS's standards, values and norms lies with the manager of each unit. The regular examinations on the psycho-social work environment are compulsory and are part of the ambition to be "a responsible and healthy organization," as one senior manager explained. But managers and supervisors also have the opportunity to contact the HO unit for specific examinations if they find that the work climate is poor. One shop floor supervisor said that

> after a steady decrease in productivity in one team, we decided that something had to be done. So we asked the health department to come to us and make an investigation into the culture of the group, and they found a lot of problems that we have been working on ever since. Now productivity has gone up to a satisfactory level again.

Overall, the link between "a good psycho-social work environment, individual health and team productivity," as one manager of the HO unit described it, is "critical for our ability to make managers understand that we have to deal with these issues seriously." As part of the SPS-logic of standardization and constant improvement, all experiences and data from the examinations of the workplaces, irrespective of whether they are done by ergonomic experts and work environment engineers, or by health promotion experts and behavioral specialists, are collected by the HO unit and discussed internally regarding the developing of new work environment standards for the entire organization. One health promotion expert said, "What we are doing in one workplace, may lead to altered standards for all workplaces, even globally." To this extent "we try to enact common principles of behavior that is conducive to good health at all of our workplaces," one HO manager said.

Overall, managers are critical to the success of the current health promotion philosophy of Scania, where "a link between health promotion programs and activities and increased productivity, quality and morale is critical," as one senior manager put it. One factory manager stressed that "it is important that you as a manager commit yourself to creating a healthy workplace, it will stimulate your employees' motivation to take active responsibility for their own and their team-mates competence and health." At the internal website of Scania, it is stressed that

> managers are expected to have a positive attitude towards the health promotion work that is carried out in the company and should organize the work in such a way that employees can regularly participate in those programs that are deemed necessary.

Managers are expected to support employees in their efforts to take "personal responsibility for their job, their career and their health." One of the managers of the HO unit said that

> today's logic emphasizes individual responsibility among our employees, that they are able to take actions when so needed by focusing deviances in the production and by suggesting improvements. The traditional industrial worker who just obeyed orders no longer exists. We want people who are committed and who have a personal drive, and who are able to work in self-managing teams. Our managers should give them the opportunity to do so, for instance, by helping them to increase their self-awareness that some of our programs make possible.

One senior manager of Scania explained that "we try to support our managers to help them develop their employees into active and entrepreneurial people, and here our health department can be a great source of inspiration, knowledge and support." A critical issue remains the notion of 'performance management.'

> What do our employees need in order to perform? Well, obviously good health is the basis for their performance. But health is not only about physiological or mental well-being. It's about commitment, joy, happiness and motivation. These are vital aspects that our managers

must think about if they are to successfully operate according to the principles and values of our production system.

The alleged gains from focusing employees' health is also emphasized during various management training programs. In the presentation of one course, it was emphasized that "a good working environment and health is a strategic issue to Scania" since it is a basic condition to develop and keep committed and motivated employees. It is said that every manager "has the responsibility for the physical, mental and social work environment" and that every employee has "a personal responsibility for his or her health and well-being." It is further emphasized that

> your health is certainly a private matter, but it is also of critical importance to the company. Your health is an important prerequisite for success both on and off the job. Your lifestyle is critical to how your health develops that affects your motivation, commitment and ability to stay alert at work.

One of the health promotion experts said that "our message on focusing on health rather than sickness is appreciated by many managers. It's not about focusing on problems, but on solutions." One of the managers of the HO unit stressed that

> most managers want to look forward, not backwards, and it's in this context that health promotion as a management practice work so well. We try to make them understand that we can be a partner to them, by offering them tools, ideas and measures on how to improve their operations.

One shop floor supervisor claimed that "I guess most of us accept the idea that a healthy workforce is a productive workforce, so we're interested in learning more about how our employees can maintain good health." One plant manager argued that "those who don't cope with the work are often those that don't care about their health." One of his colleagues stressed that "those among my employees that are healthy are often the most ambitious and productive. I guess it has to do with a combination of being in mental balance, having self-control and a good physique." A recently employed shop floor supervisor said that "the ideas of health promotion are good since they are about empowering people, rather than pointing out problems only." In a statement to new managers, one senior manager argued that

> good health goes hand in hand with efficiency and profitability. If you feel well, then you perform well, it's a simple and logical truth. At Scania we have a tradition to support our employees and their families and we believe that a health-promoting leadership is an important part of that enterprise.

He went on to say that

> health promotion and a healthy work culture is not only about reducing
> absence due to sickness; it's primarily about motivating and empower-
> ing our employees, our most important resource. Therefore health
> promotion is a strategic issue for any manager of Scania.

One factory manager further emphasized this by saying

> each and every one of us must be aware of their health. It's about your
> ability to make active decisions, e.g. to exercise even though you're not
> motivated. This philosophy can be translated to your work, where you
> need to be active and committed, even though you're perhaps not
> always motivated. Then you help yourself and your colleagues. If you
> don't want to, then no one else can do it for you.

He concluded, "I would never be able to perform as much as I do today
without a strict regime of exercise, diet and good habits." One HR-manager
emphasized "good health is about self-discipline, e.g. eating the right stuff.
These are competencies that you can use in your daily work as well." Concretely, a "health promoting leadership" can be accomplished by "identifying early signals of bad health in the organization" as one of the managers
of the HO unit explained.

Managers and supervisors are educated in "how to detect risky behavior
among the employees." This training program concerns the manager's ability to "be vigilant about potential problems among the employees in order
to maintain their health." One shop floor supervisor explained that he had
used a checklist that allowed him "to observe changes in the behavior
among his staff," where "I recognized that some had become less focused
than before. One of them didn't cope as well as previously, and another guy
had started talking speedily and so." Together with a health promotion
expert, it was concluded that these persons were suffering from "early
symptoms of stress." They were given new tasks that "were more appropriate for them" and were invited to participate in a training program of
stress management "in order to be able to cope with the job again in the
future." But a "health-promoting leadership" is "not only about promoting
concrete issues that are conducive to good health such as physical exercise,
good social relations in the work team, good sleeping and eating habits, and
so on," as one of the managers of the HO unit explained:

> It is also about promoting a value-based management where employees
> come to share Scania's values and principles. Employees that share the
> company's values won't need any advice on how to stay healthy; they
> will do this anyway, they will come to appreciate health as a critical

competence in managing their job. Ultimately, these values can become part of their lifestyle.

According to Swedish law, company doctors and company nurses in Sweden, are to be independent and neutral actors, not serving the interests of either employees or employers. One nurse said that

> there can be tricky cases where a client, i.e., a manager, has contacted us since he believes that one of his employees needs help as he for some reason or another has started behaving odd, or is in fact sick. But then it turns out that the problem may be more complicated than just the individual 'failing' to do what is expected from him according to work standards and so on; that the problem may lie in the work environment or in the manager's leadership style, or in the culture and norms of the team that the employee is part of. Managers may become upset when we come to the conclusion that the person is not sick in a medical sense or just unhealthy, but that the reasons for his behavior is to be found elsewhere. Then we can offer more group-oriented activities in order to create a healthier workplace.

A colleague of hers even expressed that

> some managers believe that we are a service unit to them, which is true to some extent, but that we should do as they tell us to do. This is a dilemma. We need a good collaboration with the managers as they are our clients, but we must also maintain our integrity and medical profession. There can be an implicit pressure on us to serve primarily the employer.

One of the nurses said that the employer has by law the responsibility for securing a good working climate in addition to achieving tough productivity goals.

> If we find out that a person abuses alcohol, we, as medical experts, are not allowed to tell the managers about this despite the fact that this may be the reason as to why the person is failing either in an ongoing rehabilitation process or at his or her ordinary job. Then we try to induce the person to be open about this. If the person is not willing to tell his or her manager, the manager may start believing that he or she is lazy, incompetent or whatever, when in fact he or she needs care and medical intervention. So it's best to be open about this, then we can help the employee, together with the manager. In this way we try to help both the employee and the employer.

One of the behavioral experts of the HO unit said that in her job, she often met managers who gave one version of a situation and employees who gave another. Often, she was contacted by managers to solve conflicts between them and their employees or between the employees.

> I can experience frustration due to the fact that I am trained to listen to both parties and not judge anyone in advance. Typically, I think that the employee is telling the truth and that the manager is also telling the truth, they just look upon a situation from different perspectives. Some managers have said that we listen too much to the employees. I understand such reactions, they expect employees to obey. But some managers expect us to be their partners in such cases, and that is problematic.

Nevertheless, one of the members of the management team of the HO unit thought that their mission was clear. She stressed that

> we should not act as the counsellor of the employee versus the employer as it was in the old days. The traditional way stipulated that 'my responsibility is the patient.' This idea is still prevailing at hospitals and ordinary medical clinics. The loyalty is towards the patient. This is a company. We believe that it is the employees who must take responsibility for their health, and our job is to support the employer to do this. This unit has a joint goal with the rest of the organization: the individual should become and remain healthy.

One of the company doctors further elaborated this by claiming

> my mission is to help the individual according to the company's needs and resources. Our job, as company doctors compared to ordinary doctors who work at a hospital is to think about the individual in his or her organizational role. At a hospital, you only see the patient and his or her problems, complaints and needs. Here we must take into consideration the social world that the individuals are part of; their teammates, their bosses, the production, and so on.

One of the nurses even said that

> it is very hard to be an independent expert unit given the fact that it is the managers of the various plants and facilities who are our customers. They are paying our salaries. In the end, we must take that into account. If there is a conflict between a manager and an employee, typically it is the employee who ends up with us in order to undergo some program of change if he or she is to remain in employment. We can't bite the hand that feeds us.

One of the plant managers stressed this new point even more clearly by claiming that

> the medical guys are great since they can help me communicate better with my employees. I can tell them about a problem I have, e.g. regarding speed of operations. For instance, recently we had to increase speed in order to meet new production goals. Then, some of our employees started lagging behind. This issue is quite common, and the subject of occasional complaint and dissatisfaction at the shop floor. In conversations with HO personnel I explained to them why we can't reduce the pace, it's about competition, economy, and all that. It's not an issue of negotiation. Instead we have to find solutions of how to help people to cope with it, e.g. by designing good workplaces together with HO's work environment engineers, promoting good health through physical exercise programs, and so on. Sometimes they need just to talk to the employees, they have their medical arguments you know. The HO unit is a means through which we can secure the SPS. Of course I listen to them if they raise strong objections to my plans and ideas and sometimes I have to change my mind. Overall, however, I believe they are not rigid but see their role in our quest to detect deviances and make continued improvements.

Another manager at a plant witnessed that

> our medical department is very helpful. When we see that a person can't cope, is making a lot of mistakes, stays at home or whatever sign of failing, then we can contact them. We have occasionally staff here that is sick a lot, then it's great that we have a department that can make an evaluation of their status from the company's point-of-view. The health guys are also a great resource in complex rehabilitation issues where I lack competence, they know how to help people return to work, or they can help us explain to the individual why he should try to find another work, if it proves that he can't cope any longer.

In these cases, the HO unit offers a set of services by their different work teams that include various professionals. One company nurse said that

> in many cases, health problems may be complex and may require the competence of both a doctor and a psychologist and a health promotion expert. Thanks to our teams, we are able to approach many aspects of an individual's behavior that are not even necessarily related to his or her work only.

The need for company doctors and other members of the HO of being loyal to Scania's managers is further emphasized by the fact that HO's activities are dependent on their legitimacy. One of the members of the management team of HO expressed that

> the reason as to why we have been able to grow extensively during the years is our skill in marketing ourselves to the rest of the company, thus creating a need for us among managers. Most managers look upon us as their close ally in securing a smooth and efficient production, as resources for helping them prevent problems and solving problems.

One of the employees, a company nurse claimed,

> you know, this is a commercial activity inside a company that operates in a highly competitive environment. We need to sell our services and make ourselves attractive, otherwise we will end up unemployed. Top management can accept that we may not be profitable as they look upon us as a mechanism of achieving a healthy and well-operating organization, but we must not make any fuzz, we are there to serve and support.

One of the HO managers recounted that he had to move one company doctor that was working at a plant, since the managers there were not pleased with him.

> He was appreciated by the employees, but he didn't get along very well with the managers, and since they are our clients, we had to do something about it. Contrary to a general hospital where it would be very hard for a single patient to demand the replacement of a doctor, we are in a business organization where other rules prevail. Doctors here are not at the top of the ladder. They are expected to help managers run their business.

One of the company nurses pointed out,

> you can't be too idealistic. When I started here, I always focused on what was best for the employee, ignoring the needs of the company. That didn't work out very well. I learned to balance the need of the organization to the need of the individual.

Accordingly, one of her colleagues argued that

> back in the old days, when we were only a small medical unit, we weren't that concerned about the operations of the company. We attended to problems among individuals, nothing more. Now

we are expected to think about company needs and performance in our decision making. We are after all a company health unit.

This philosophy should embrace all levels of the organization, where company doctors are expected to be concerned both about the medical status of a person, and his or her role and behavior in the organization. The company doctor who is responsible for the medical examinations of Scania's top managers said that

> previously these encounters concerned medical issues only, like screening for cholesterol and so on. Today, the medical part is only 25 percent of the time spent together. Most of the time we talk about organizational issues, and this has given me an understanding of the challenges of the company and the requirements of each and everyone.

At her disposal to make analyses of the organization's need is a so-called organization psychologist employed by the HO. "This person helps me to better see each person's function in a larger system so that I can make better diagnoses and suggestions of treatment." She emphasized that

> our managers need to perform all the time, and therefore they need to pursue a healthy lifestyle in order to cope with the demands put on them. In this way my job relates closely to SPS. Hopefully, I am not only helping our top managers to develop as individuals; I am also helping them run this organization in a better way.

According to one ergonomic expert, the ability to influence the mindset and behavior of employees is closely related to her role as an independent professional.

> Compared to people working in our human resource organization who are generally seen as representatives for the employer, we are seen as experts who are there to help them to improve their work environment. This gives us a unique position in the company.

This experience was shared by a company doctor who thought that

> employees appreciate what we do; we are the concrete manifestation of a company that cares. Being a physician creates a platform for trustful relations and communication. People can be open about things to us that they may resort from being in other relations, and we can communicate issues to them that may be harder for managers or other persons in this company to do. In this way I think we have power even in relation to our clients [the managers], and we must use that power in a responsible manner.

Indeed, much of the work being done by members of the HO organization is

> about building trustful relations with the rest of the organization, then
> our job will run smoothly. We need to create a climate of trust, based
> on mutual respect and where it is possible for us to discuss cases openly
> and frankly. Long-term relations are critical for our ability to get jobs
> internally. Managers tend to contact those nurses and doctors with
> whom they are familiar and feel confident about. We need to work in
> an active way, make ourselves known, show them what we can help
> them with, suggest solutions, and so on. In traditional medical care,
> people are reactive, waiting for patients to come to them. We can't just
> do that.

Making contact with managers is mostly about spreading ideas that have
been generated internally at HO, e.g. the need for plant managers to "create
a healthy organization," as one of the employees said.

> The concept of 'healthy organization' is linked to an idea of a high-
> performing organization that can be accomplished through behavioral
> changes among the employees concerning, e.g. their sleeping habits,
> diet, leisure activities, and, of course, how they conduct their work.
> This is generally an attractive idea for managers.

Thus, in their contacts with plant managers, employees of HO offer various
programs in terms of training, education, and so on, to accomplish an
organization "that performs even better," as one of the HO managers put it.
Overall,

> it is extremely important that we are present in the organization
> through our activities and that people are aware of us. This is the only
> way we can communicate our ideas on health and well-being, and how
> they can add to the bottom line.

Irrespective of whether the HO unit interacts with the employees at regular medical examinations at the HO unit, during rehabilitation processes,
or through other activities, much knowledge has been generated. For
instance, all encounters between health professionals from the HO unit and
the employees and managers are documented and systematized in accordance with the medical tradition of setting up case records. This ambition is
closely linked to the SPS's focus on visualization and transparency, where all
problems and potential risks in the organization is to be brought to the
surface in order to take corrective actions and make appropriate improvements. Case records of each employee regarding his or her health; of each
work team, unit and factory gives the members of the HO unit a unique
knowledge of the mental and social status of Scania as a company. The

"health status" of particular units, teams and even individuals (in the case of specific rehabilitation processes) is presented with considerable details with a view to maintaining or increasing Scania's productivity. What is peculiar about this statistical enterprise is that "no link between increased health and increased productivity and improved quality has been shown," as the manager of the HO unit explained. But,

> there is a significant management dimension to this, where our unit can serve top management with detailed data on issues that our regular personnel departments don't have access to. People's health serves as indicators of their ability to work according to the management principles in operation.

Concretely, data from all interaction between the HO unit and the rest of Scania is regularly analyzed by the health teams. For example, in one of the teams discussions revolved around obesity among the personnel at one of the factories and various suggestions on how to approach this issue was debated. The discussion was based on statistics from the HO unit's medical department and its regular medical screening of personnel. At these screenings, it was detected that many employees at one specific plant exceeded 'a normal body mass index,' i.e., 25 according to the norms set by the World Health Organization. It was decided that contact should be made to the manager of the unit in order to propose a weight-training program for those exceeding a body mass index of 25.

Hence, it is through the knowledge the HO unit generates about Scania's operations and personnel that the HO has the potential to affect not only issues relating to employees' health and well-being, but also the general management of Scania. These 'managerial powers' of the HO appear, in turn, to be related to how the knowledge and expertise it holds provides it with unique abilities of handling a number of delicate issues that no other unit within Scania can rightfully handle. One of these concern how Scania can further employees' health and well-being, while, at once, furthering the efficiency of Scania's operations. An environmental engineer said that

> sometimes there is no conflict between these two goals. Yet, sometimes there is, and that is where our job becomes a little bit more complicated. Over the years I think that the HO has proven that we understand and respect that balance; we have shown the people upstairs that we know how far we can go in our pursuit of furthering individuals' health and well-being.

One of the managers of the HO commented on the same issue:

> We must have an immediate and almost intuitive understanding for how far and in which directions we can go in our pursuits of caring for

the health of Scania's employees. Scania is a competitive business corporation that strives to make a profit. It is our task to develop organizational and technical solutions which, at least in the long run, furthers Scania's business without jeopardizing the health of our employees, or even better, to develop organizational solutions that further the health of our employees and Scania's business.

In this connection, it is only the health teams within the HO that can legitimately claim to know how to deal with this tricky balance. A human resource manager in one of Scania's units said that "no other unit within Scania has the knowledge to legitimately have a say about both the health and the technical efficiency of the operations." This claim was confirmed by one of the senior managers of Scania:

> Not only line managers and personnel, but also managers higher up in the organizational hierarchy listen to the suggestions of the HO. I mean the HO constitutes a centre of expertise in all areas that concern the relations between the health and well-being of our employees and our production and business principles. It would not be wise to disregard their opinion; especially since we even say in the official presentation of the SPS that one of Scania's basic values is 'respect for the individual.'

Through their legitimate ability to speak in the name of both the health of the personnel and the efficiency of Scania, the multi-professional teams within the HO appear to have a unique position in the general management of Scania. This position seems to be furthered by the legitimacy of the teams to handle another delicate issue, which concerns the relation between employees' lifestyles and the professional abilities of the employees. With the introduction of the SPS, it has become increasingly clear that the ways in which employees live their lives outside work is not insignificant for their performance at work. That is, the extent to which employees are fit or not for the active and social forms of work that the SPS imply is generally seen to be a question not merely of professional competencies and the efforts the employees put in to improve these competencies during the work day. It is also seen as a question of what the employee do after the work day has ended. Especially through the physicians, the behavioral therapists, and the health promotion specialists, the teams have the ability to pass beyond the professional sphere into what would have been for a HR manager or any other kind of manager a sphere in which they would have neither jurisdiction nor expertise. As said by a HR manager:

> Sometimes when one of your employees has problems, you kind of sense that it is not work related, but concerns problems the employee has with his wife or with his children. We cannot and should not deal with that, because then we would pass a threshold that I think should

not be passed. Some of the professionals at the HO can do that, however. It is in fact part of their job.

A line manager made a similar comment:

> Some of the problems our employees have in coping with their jobs are not job related. The HO can help us and the employees in those cases. They can give the employees therapy; coach them in their pursuits of living healthier and feeling better about themselves, and so on.

Hence, the HO is a source of influence in the general management of Scania's procedures. It does not merely react and deal with concrete health problems and accidents, but can also take initiatives and act on risks related to accidents that have not yet occurred or potential gains in motivation, in physical or psychological well-being, which are yet to be realized. Yet, the HO's influence on managerial decisions does not merely derive from this ability to take proactive initiatives; it derives in addition from how the ability to act on risks and potentials drastically expands its potential clientele. As said by a physician with a special responsibility for developing the statistical expertise of the HO:

> We have to try to develop a general and statistically certified knowledge about how different ways of organizing work affects the health and efficiency of Scania's employees. If we do that I think that we can significantly influence how things are organized here. Because then, we can use our expertise to suggest changes which concern not only those who are ill or injured but the rest of the personnel as well.

7 Practices and Procedures in Managing Health

In this chapter, we turn to the specific programs and services that the HO provides, in order to better understand the effects that they may bring about among the employees. As reported earlier, Scania's health policy is conceptualized into three programs: (a) red, i.e., rehabilitation and restoration of sickness and illness; (b) yellow, i.e., prevention of sickness and illness; and (c) green, i.e., promoting health. Some of the activities and programs that the HO devises can certainly be categorized as 'red' because they are offered only when there are some concrete and immediate health problems that require care; all these activities and programs are also contrived to function as instruments that can help to prevent general categories of health problems from reoccurring. Furthermore, all activities and programs that can be categorized as 'yellow' because they are offered as instruments for the prevention of health problems and risks are also meant as instruments for revealing concrete and immediate health problems. Hence, red and yellow activities and programs are interrelated in a circular movement, where the one tends to lead to the other. The 'green' activities and programs are somewhat idiosyncratic because their point of departure is different; green activities and programs are neither set off by some concrete and immediate health problems, nor by some screening for early signs of what may in the long run develop into such health problems, but by a belief in the potential of improving individuals' general state of health, well-being and efficiency.

The most concrete example of a red activity takes place when an employee reports in sick and therefore is unable to come to work. The HO then provides a so-called health dialogue service. Traditionally, when employees are sick they have reported this to the person directly over them in the formal hierarchy. With the health dialogue service, the Scania employees instead report in sick to a nurse at the HO. The nurse documents not only the name of the employee, but also why he or she reports in sick. Furthermore, the nurse asks the employee a set of more specific questions about the symptoms of the illness and gives various advice as to how the employee should handle the illness. This process is repeated the third day of the employees' absenteeism and again on the eighth day. Through this process the intention is, on the one hand, to provide the employee with an immediate professional response that may help the employee in his or her self-care. On the other hand, it is to provide the HO with information about specific individuals' illnesses, which can then be added to its general statistical knowledge about absenteeism. A nurse explained that

> basically, the health dialogue is a way of keeping track of employees' absenteeism, both on the individual and on the organizational level. This knowledge is useful in so many ways. It lets us know which of our individual employees have specific health problems such as shoulder, neck and back problems, stomach problems, sleeping disorders, etc. By providing this information to our statisticians we can also learn more about what groups of employees have these problems, where these groups work, how they live, how old they are, if they are primarily men or women, if they are slim or overweight, and so on.

By providing this information, the health dialogue service also helps the HO in its work with yellow health activities, i.e., with prevention of illnesses and injuries. A nurse further argued that

> the health dialogue service helps us monitor health risks, both on the individual and on the group level. By keeping detailed accounts of all employees who report in sick we can often detect risks of long-term sick absenteeism very early and take various measures. For instance, if an employee reports in sick on several occasions because of back problems we make an appointment with this employee and start investigating the matter further. The employee might need to start doing weight training or maybe he or she should stop doing something, on the job or at home. In any event, the health dialogue service helps us keep track of these things and also helps us suggest measures at very early stages of what could otherwise lead to a deteriorating process.

The health dialogue service is generally seen as a simple and efficient instrument for generating a lot of information about employees concerning not only the specific illnesses that caused the employee to report in sick, but also information about their general health status and lifestyle.

> If we notice that an employee has reported in sick on several occasions and that it always is the same problem, then we start digging a little deeper to try to see if there are any underlying factors that cause the illnesses. We may ask about sleeping and eating habits, and possibly even drinking habits—although the latter may be a little sensitive.

The process of reaching the decision to propose the Regional Insurance Offices to eventually sick-list an individual at Scania is done by the HO, and this unit acts as a resource for the managers and supervisors in charge of the sick person to return to work. Depending on the reasons for the sick-listing, regular meetings with the employee, his or her manager and a representative from the HO unit are held. Rehabilitation meetings are about managing the rehabilitation process according to a medical plan, "where we try to investigate the possibilities for the person to return," as a company doctor said. During a rehabilitation process sometimes only a company doctor is present as representative from the HO unit, sometimes a complete health team consisting of nurses, doctors, health promotion experts and so on, is involved. Each rehabilitation process is to be formally conducted according to Scania's health policy, i.e., involving both restorative practices in terms of, e.g. work training, medication, hospitalization, training by physiotherapists, talks with psychologists, etc., in order to deal with the existing problem; as well as health promoting activities in order to address hazards in the person's lifestyle that may lead to future sick-listing. A company doctor said, "previously we only looked at the existing status of the person and what should be done to help him or her, but nowadays we are more proactive in the sense of figuring out what might happen in the future." One employee, who previously had been sick-listed due to a broken arm, recalled that she was encouraged to make a health profile examination. Together with a health promotion expert, an agreement was made that she would participate in an education on diet in order to deal with mild obesity that potentially could cause problems in the future. One of the managers of the HO unit said that,

> in whatever activity we are involved we try to address how this organization can become healthier by preventing diseases and maintaining good health, therefore the rehabilitation process must not only deal with already existing problems but also look at preventing risks or strengthening what is already fine.

During rehabilitation (for whatever reason), each employee is asked to fill out a form on lifestyle and habits. A company nurse stressed:

> Even though a person is on sick-listing due to pregnancy, this is a good opportunity to check on the status of a person's habits concerning sleep, smoking, exercise, and so on. In this way we can advise the person on how to maintain good health or help him or her to become in better shape, irrespective of the reasons for his or her current sick-listing.

As a general rule, employees who have reported in ill five times in a year have the right—and the obligation—to take part in a "health talk." Depending on the type of health problems the individual has, the health talk is handled by a nurse, physician or health promotion expert. Furthermore, apart from the employee, it also involves the employees' first line superior. A physician explained:

> the health talks are examples of activities that are located precisely between the red, and the yellow category, because, on the one hand, they are meant to help the employee with the health problems he or she presently has. On the other hand, however, they are also meant to prevent the reoccurrence of these and other health problems in the future.

The health talks are handled as relatively informal discussions. A behavioral expert specified what issues may be brought up during the health talks:

- What are your work tasks?
- How long have you been working for Scania and at your unit?
- Do you have irregular working hours?
- How many members does your work team consist of?
- Is the atmosphere good in the team?
- Can you ask your colleagues for advice?
- Do you enjoy your work?
- What annoys you at work?
- Do you see your colleagues off the job?
- Do you have good relations with your supervisor?
- Does your supervisor listen to you?
- Do you get credit for what you do at work?
- Do you regularly propose solutions for improvements? Are they taken into account?
- When you have been absent, where have you been?
- Do you exercise?
- How do you spend your leisure time?
- Do you smoke?
- What are your eating habits?
- What are your sleeping habits?
- Do you have a family?
- Are you lonely?
- Do you experience stress?
- Where do you live?
- Do you enjoy life?
- Do you eat any medication?
- Do you have any personal goals?
- What do you want to do with your life?

The health talks aim to help the expert, the employee and the employee's superior to put the employee's attitudes and behaviors into a wider explanatory context in terms of existing or potential health risks. Ideally, the health talks should be led by the employees' own free presentation about their health status, work and private life in order to make them more committed to the results of these talks. This was seen as important because motivation to improve and to change "is sometimes an important part of the health problem itself," as one of the behavioral experts said. A company nurse claimed: "We cannot tell them to change the way they live; they have to make the changes themselves. That is why it is so important to help them come to the conclusion that they need to make changes on their own." Finally, the idea of letting the employees' superior take part in these sessions is to give him or her better information about the employees' alleged health risks so that he or she can better cope with his or her responsibility of keeping the work environment safe and beneficiary to employees' performance. As said by a line manager,

> if I know more about my employees' situation, here at work, at home, or wherever, it is easier for me to make the right decisions. We try to work according to the principles of the SPS where things should be transparent; we should not brush things underneath the carpet.

When the health talks concern sociopsychological issues, such as different forms of stress, they often lead to further sessions with a behavioral therapist. The HO has observed a steady increase in psycho-social problems in general and stress-related problems in particular. It is especially among white-collar employees that such problems have increased. For these reasons, the HO decided in 2007 to put together a group of therapists informally designated as the "psycho-social team." One of the members of this team explained that "we believe that the underlying causes of the increase in stress-related problems among white-collar employees relate to difficulties in setting formal and temporal limits around their work and responsibilities." A therapist developed this point. He said,

> even though it is not said officially, a company such as Scania operates according to sub-optimization principle. What I mean by this is simply that our qualified white-collar employees tend to have more to do than they are able to handle, at least if they want to do their job carefully and well. So they have to prioritize; they have to be able to judge which assignments they should handle with special care and attention, and which assignments they should not invest too much time and effort into. If you cannot make those judgements, and if you find it difficult to accept the fact that some of the work that carries your name cannot be carried out in accordance with what you and others consider to be your normal standards, you risk running into 'the wall.'

In relation to these issues, several professionals within the HO emphasized that the possibilities of changing the organization is generally very limited. A therapist said that we can help by temporarily limiting the responsibilities and the performance criteria of those employees who come to us with stress problems. Yet, in the long run either these employees learn to cope with their work or try to find other less demanding work.

Hence, the focus of the therapeutic sessions is the individual, and the aim is to teach the individual to adapt to work rather than the other way round. Put differently, the problem, or at least the part of the problem that the therapist seeks to do something about, is found at the individual level, not at the organizational level; it is the individuals' lack of abilities to cope with stress and to set limits and prioritize that is at the center of the therapists' attention. An employee who had taken therapy for her stress problems elaborated on this point:

> About a year ago I was on the verge of crossing a line where things would have begun to fall apart. It was actually my boss who acknowledged the state I was in and suggested that I should seek help. To step aside for a while and to receive therapy proved to be both necessary and helpful. It has helped me look at myself, my work and my life with some perspective. Before I was so completely occupied by my work, now I am able to keep some distance. It has also helped me to cope better with stress. Yet, at times I still feel a little bit bitter, because throughout the whole process we never discussed how the organization in which I work could or should be changed. It was I who had a problem, it was within me, and in the ways I related to and handled my work that the problems were to be found, not in the work that I was set to do. So I felt that it was I who had to admit that I was not able to cope with the work that I was employed to do.

In line with this statement, the first step in the therapy is to establish a trustful climate that helps the employee to accept and commit to 'the fact' that he or she has a problem with stress. A therapist said that

> daring to be open and honest about the fact that you do have a problem is very important; because stress has a lot to do with an experience of not being able to meet expectations, not at least those expectations that you take on yourself. Declaring openly that you have a problem relieves you of some of that burden, at least momentarily, and gives you the opportunity to be honest towards yourself and to accept that you have a problem.

In the long run however, it was emphasized that it was obviously not enough for the employee just to be open and honest about his or her problems to the therapist and to him or herself. The employee also should be open to his or her colleagues and supervisors as part of the transparent culture of SPS, where all members of a team participate in 'continuous improvements' by detecting and correcting 'deviances.' The therapist continued:

we try to involve employees' superiors in the therapy after some sessions, because if there is no understanding and acceptance for an individual employees' problems the risk is that things will be just like they were before the problems surfaced and became acute.

However, this approach can be somewhat problematic since it can jeopardize the career prospects of the employee. A therapist explained that

the problem with this approach is that the capability to work under pressure and to cope with stress and uncertainty are core features of SPS. To openly declare, even in front of your boss, that you cannot cope with the stress will be seen by many as a way of saying that you are no longer in the race, and thus, that you are not a 'Scania person.'

An employee who had taken therapy for a couple of months because of stress problems commented on this issue. She said:

At some point I had to admit, not the least to myself that I could no longer cope; otherwise I would probably have fallen apart. I received therapy and I was helped by the therapist to discuss with my boss how my work could be changed so that it would be less stressful. For me, this was necessary, but the price I had to pay was relatively high; because now no one sees me as a person with much chance of advancing career-wise, at least not here at Scania.

Following the standard operating procedures of the SPS where detection and corrections of errors and deviances through visualization and transparency are key, the second step in the therapy revolves around mapping out the daily routines of the employee. These mapping procedures do not only concern how the employee handles his or her work, but also the private part of the employees' lives. A psychologist stressed:

The term 'the 24 hour employee' means that Scania takes an interest in and cares for its employees not only here at work, but also in their lives outside work. This is not merely a question of being nice and caring. Scania's executives know that the ways in which employees live outside work significantly affect their abilities and their efficiency at work.

On the basis of such a map of the individuals' daily routines, before, during and after work, the therapy begins. One of the therapists explained:

sometimes the therapy is relatively straightforward and concrete. When I look at an employee's daily routines I might find that everything is a mess. Just straightening things out a little bit, suggesting for instance that the employee contacts someone who can help with cleaning the house and washing the clothes once a week may change a lot. Generally, just because an individual has shown signs of severe stress you should not automatically assume that an employee has fundamental psychological problems that need to be handled by a therapist.

Sometimes, however, the problems are more complicated and require more extensive therapy. In some of these cases, employees are given the opportunity to take part in another service that the HO provides, the so-called Health School. The Health School was established in 2002 by two members of the HO's management team and is specifically devoted to treating employees who have problems with stress and run the risk of ending up in long-term absenteeism. As explained by the manager of the Health School:

> the people who come here are in the risk zone. You can say that they are in-between the red and the yellow category. Our programs are specifically designed to help people with stress problems at very early stages, hopefully before their problems make them incapacitated.

There are several different pathways that lead to the Health School. Mostly, the clients of the Health School have been in contact with a behavioral therapist at the HO who has seen the Health School as a good solution to the clients' problems. Another pathway goes via the individual health profile investigations that the HO carries out (see later). Sometimes the Health School is also contacted directly by an employee's manager. The manager of the Health School said that

> generally managers are today very aware of the importance of looking out for signs of ill-health such as fatigue, short-term absence, concentration difficulties, etc. It is also officially declared that it is the managers' responsibility to be watchful about such matters.

Once an individual has become a client or 'student' of the Health School, he or she takes part, first, in a six-week program and then in a follow-up program that stretches over a period of one year. During the six-week program, the client 'goes to school' Monday to Friday, between 8 a.m. and 12 noon and then either works part-time or not at all. In the follow-up program that involves a limited number of meetings, the client is supposed to work full-time again. In the introduction to the programs, the professionals of the Health School meet with the client and the client's boss to discuss the client's problems and the purpose of the program. This constellation rejoins in a new meeting after the first six-week program. At this point, the professions discuss the results of the first part of the program with the client and his or her superior, and draws up the lines for the clients' continued health work. In the follow-up program, the client should be equipped with enough skills and self-esteem to work independently with the stress issues that brought him or her to the Health School. Follow-up meetings are held with a therapist about once every 6 to 8 weeks and the program is ended after one year with a final meeting between the client, the behavioral therapist and the client's superior.

A therapist at the Health School explained that the underlying therapeutic method that it uses is based on the idea of teaching individuals to manage early signs of stress by giving them better "self-knowledge" and abilities to maintain "a dialogue with their selves."

> We try to teach them how to control their own lives and selves. But it all has to start with them accepting that they are responsible for their lives; they have to accept that they are no victims and that they always have a choice.

She went on to argue that many clients

> initially tend to place their problems outside themselves. Their job is seen as too demanding; or the boss is unable to set realistic and clear goals and performance standards. We try to turn that around. We want them to see that the problem and the solution lie within themselves.

Hence, the idea of individual responsibility is emphasized by the Health School's program. A colleague of hers said that "we create stress ourselves and it is therefore our responsibility to do something about it." Clients are taught to deal with stress, not only by being more aware and reflective about their own behavior and attitudes, but also by starting to think in strategic terms, not just about their work, but about all areas of their lives.

> Clients are taught to make distinctions between work, private life and self, and to set goals in all three areas. It is a mindset that we want our clients to adopt. They should be aware of what they are doing and they should think in terms of how the different areas of life, work, private life and self, relate to one another.

Generally, the professionals at the Health School did not disregard the fact that the professional environment in which the clients worked could be more or less pressing for the clients. On the contrary, this was more or less taken for granted by them. Yet, it was seen to lie beyond their ambition and beyond their mission to suggest and possibly to implement new organizational solutions that would change these conditions. In this respect, the professional environment of the clients was basically treated as given, i.e., as something that profoundly affected the clients' health and well-being, but that the clients and the Health School could not change; they could only learn to adapt to and cope with it. A therapist explained that ultimately we do try to teach them how to cope with their life and their work here at Scania, we teach them to listen to themselves, we teach them to choose, and to accept the fact that in the final instance it is they themselves that are responsible for their health and well-being.

In addition to the Health School, the HO offers sessions on various health topics, such as physical exercise, stress, drugs and alcohol, smoking, and similar issues that are claimed to be important when trying to promote health. During one of these occasions, a group of 40 employees listened to one of the HO unit's dietary experts who gave advice on how to eat properly; what kind of mix of food; how much; how often; and so on. She stressed that "employees that are health conscious take responsibility for their health and well-being and contribute to a good quality of life for themselves and their colleagues, low rates of absence and thus high productivity." According to her, it's important "to make smart choices and it's up to you if you want to remain fit and healthy and can continue to contribute." In a similar way, a program called "The Force of the Mind" emphasized each employee's personal responsibility for maintaining "a positive and constructive approach." In a document describing this course, it was stressed that "you can choose what you're thinking about, the course helps you choose thoughts that can help you stay healthy and alert." In general, the courses are about inducing each employee to feel responsibility for his or her health, well-being and lifestyle. One of the managers of the HO unit explained:

> A general principle for all our courses is that they should help the employee to answer two questions: '1. This is how I feel today' and '2. This is how I want to feel tomorrow.' The employees decide themselves their level of ambition and their possible lifestyle change. The courses can show what is possible, but it's up to each individual to do something about his or her current health.

Much of the information that is given during the courses is also available at the internal website of Scania, where advice is given on food and diet, physical exercise, how to cope with stress, etc. This information "can be seen as an easy way for our employees to become aware of their responsibility for maintaining a healthy lifestyle, as well as a way for our unit to show our competencies," as the manager said.

As noted earlier, employees are involved in 'green' health activities and programs, not because they have some health problem or because they are exposed to definable risks, but because there is a belief in the potential of improving employees' general state of health, well-being, and efficiency. In this pursuit, the HO must first of all succeed in generating or tapping into the motivation and free will of the employees to get involved in the green activities and programs that it offers. A health therapist explained that we have to recruit participants to our green offerings through different forms of marketing initiatives. There are basically two reasons for this. First of all, we cannot force anyone to take part; we cannot tell employees to start eating differently or to do some kind of sport activity that we offer; they have to choose them themselves. So with our offers we compete for their time and their interest against all the other things they are offered—watching TV, going to a bar, buying chips and candy, and so on. Second, people have to come to us because they really want to, otherwise none of our offerings will have any long-term effects anyway.

Even though no one is obliged to get involved in green activities and programs, one employee underlined that

> playing sports, eating well, being outdoors, and in general, taking care of your health has almost become a norm here. I mean, it is great to be offered so many opportunities to improve your health, but you also do feel that you are expected to use these opportunities to stay fit, to prevent injuries, and to try to keep your illness absenteeism as low as possible.

Another employee pointed out that "we are quite often informed about our responsibility to take care of ourselves. I think the policies about employeeship and the 24 hour employee concern precisely this." Through a combination of offering attractive programs and facilities and launching various marketing campaigns, the HO seeks at once to appeal to the motivation and free will of its employees and to establish norms and ideals that push employees to become self-aware, health-seeking individuals who can perform effectively according to the principles and values of the SPS. A behavioral therapist said: "We try to make the employees really interested in taking care of their health and we also try to establish a culture at Scania that makes them feel that they should be active in taking care of their health."

Specifically, there are three different categories of green programs and activities. First, there are a number of health investigations. These range from restricted investigations of the eating or exercise habits of employees to investigations that seek to capture the employees' overall lifestyles. Second, there are, as already suggested, a number of courses that the employees can participate in. These also range from courses with a restricted focus on healthy eating to courses with a wide focus on all the issues involved in the notion of healthy lifestyles. Third, there are a number of therapeutic programs and activities with the same focus as the other two categories. The idea underlying these three categories is that the investigations should provide the HO as well as the employees with information about which specific areas the employees need education or possibly, therapy or coaching. That is, on paper, the investigations should establish the foundation and the point of departure for the second and third category of programs and activities. This, however, does not mean that employees are first investigated, that they then are offered specific courses, and then, if necessary, that they are offered coaching or therapy. In practice, an employee may well take a course or receive therapy without having first gone through some form of health examination.

A popular activity which sorts within the first category is the health profile investigation. In 2008 the HO carried out about 2,000 individual health profiles. That is, about 20 percent of all employees had their health profiles outlined during this year. They are commissioned by the managers of each unit and are marketed by the HO unit as "an effective management practice for developing your personnel." The health profile investigation documents an employee's general characteristics such as age, weight, height, etc., and measures general medical data such as cholesterol, blood pressure and so on. Furthermore, it maps an employee's daily habits with regard to work, eating, exercise, family life, social life and sleeping. As said by a health promotion expert:

> the health profile investigations are very encompassing. They give us detailed information about individual employees which help us suggest various forms of programs that focus precisely on those areas where an individual can and should alter his or her life.

After having discussed the results with a health promotion expert, "an agreement should be made on what to do," as one of the health experts said. Such an agreement may involve physical exercise programs geared toward losing weight, counselling with a psychologist or a behavioral expert or a talk with a nutrition specialist. The agreement is made up as a contract, signed by the employee and his or her manager as part of the individual's yearly competence development plan. After six to twelve months, a new health profile is done in order to "check on the progress being made." All health profile examinations are done individually and, as has already been suggested, there is an individual analysis carried out by a health promotion expert. In addition, results are aggregated to the team level, where they are discussed in the "improvement groups" consistent with the SPS methodology. "Some measures that need to be taken are more effective collectively rather than individually," as one of the HO unit's managers said. For instance, in one of the work teams consisting of eight persons working with sales, a meeting was held to discuss the results of the group's health profile examinations. One major theme was of particular concern to the health promotion expert, namely "the relatively high rate of divorces," which was seen as an indicator of an inability to "nurture and preserve long-lasting relations." The health promotion expert insisted on the "importance of managing these crises well" and offered talks with behavioral experts and psychologists. "We know that singles and divorced people live a more stressful life, and we want to help them cope with the anxiety and stress of going through a divorce." Besides offering counselling, she also suggested that the divorced persons should "engage themselves in any of Scania's leisure activities, where you can meet new friends and build developing networks." A colleague of hers said that

> when finding out that a person or a team suffers from poor relations either at work or at home, then you try to offer them guidance and coaching in order to return to a normal social life. It's in their interest and in the company's. People who live stable lives tend to live longer, are healthier, and more motivated and committed to work.

The reason as to why the results from the health profiles are aggregated to the group level is that "the members of the team can support each other in carrying out a change," e.g. by collectively participating in a physical exercise program in order to deal with obesity. A supervisor said that "most of the work is carried out in the group, thus it's natural that even health promotion programs are done together." One employee, a member of an administrative unit, participated together with four of his colleagues in a program on stress reduction. He explained that

> several of us have a very hectic job, and it was great to learn that you're not the only one to suffer from stress. Now we can help each other towards working in a healthier way and in trying to better cope with the 'life puzzle.'

According to one of the health promotion experts, all health profile examinations are an important part of the SPS "as they help us build a company that works on constantly improving each person's competence, lifestyle and well-being." One human resource manager explained that "health profiles help our employees to strengthen their skills about themselves, it's part of their competence development." As such, all quantitative data from the employees health profiles are aggregated to the company level in order to "detect health risks on a global basis" as one of the managers of the HO unit said. "We put together the results from the ongoing health profiles in order to see the major trends and challenges." He explained that "in the production units, problems primarily concern fatigue and sometimes poor morale," while among the research units and the administrative units, "stress and conflicts" were more common. Based on the data gathered, new training programs, e.g. sleep management and conflict resolutions, can be developed in order in order to "empower and strengthen the commitment and motivation of our employees."

As has already been suggested, a health profile examination involves both data on the physical status of the individual, as well as data on his or her relations both on and off the job. One of the managers of the HO unit stressed that "health profiles are not as restricted as regular medical screening, they are much broader in scope. They emphasize well-being and lifestyle, and therefore it is relevant to include an analysis of a person's total life." One health promotion expert said that "'balance in life' not only includes good work relations, but also good relations at home. If a person suffers from stress at Scania, if he or she has a reduced productivity, then the reasons for this may be found outside the company." A manager at the HO unit explained that

> Scania has always included the family in one way or another, e.g. by offering them participation in our leisure activities or through free visits to our primary care department. Health profiles offer an additional way for us to come closer to each employee's family by learning about his or her private life, it's a great way not only to address health hazards among the employees, but also to build a community.

Depending on what the health profile investigation shows, employees are then recommended to take part in some health course or in some form of coaching or therapy program. One example of the latter is the so-called *Scania BMI* (Body Mass Index) program. A health promotion expert explained that

> people's body weight tends to be a very sensitive issue so we are careful when we recruit people to this program. I mean, it is quite obvious that there is a general societal pressure on people today to stay slim, healthy and good-looking. These ideals and norms help us generate more interest in the BMI program. Yet, they can also make the BMI program threatening and provocative to some people. So we have to be careful. We can use these societal ideals and norms to make as many employees as possible interested and motivated. At the same time we have to make sure that employees are not offended or come to this program just because they feel the pressure; because we only want to recruit employees who come to us freely and who are motivated.

If a person has a concrete health problem that relates to the person's weight, it is of course possible for a physician or nurse to point this out and—depending on the causes of the weight problem—to suggest a diet or an exercise program. However, the BMI program is not intended for this group of individuals; rather it targets those individuals who are healthy, at least from a clinical point of view, i.e., people who have no diagnosed sign of illness, but who still want to become healthier, lose weight, look and feel better, etc.

The first step in the BMI program is an interview with the applicant. The interview is held by a health promotion expert and its purpose is twofold: to determine how motivated the applicant is and to get a grip on the eating and exercise habits of the applicant. The expert continued:

> the applicants should not only be motivated, they should also have the right motivation. Quite a lot of people are very motivated to begin eating better, to start exercising, etc., but they have no self-discipline. They are motivated and ready to subordinate to the directives that we give them, but they cannot give themselves these directives. And that is precisely what they must be able to do; because otherwise the whole program will just be a waste of time.

The eating and exercise habits of the applicant are outlined in order to design a program, which is uniquely adapted to the specific characteristics of the applicant.

> We try to put together a complete program that involves diet, exercises, stress coping routines, and so on. Most important, however, is to make our participants aware of how important these issues are; that they can do something about their lifestyle, that change is possible, and that it is their responsibility to bring about this change. They have to start thinking and acting responsibly when it comes to eating, sleeping and exercising. We can help them get on their way, but it is they themselves who have to change.

The BMI program is not only a specific instrument for making employees eat better and, when necessary, to lose weight, it is also a general instrument for making the employee reflect upon the choices he or she makes in life and work, always with the intention of changing things for the better.

In cases where therapy or counselling is recommended, a number of examinations are undertaken in order to help the employee better manage his or her overall lifestyle. First, the historical events and initiatives that have led to the employees' present situation in work and life are outlined and analyzed.

> At this point we help the employee describe for him or herself how he or she lives on a day-to-day basis; what kind of work he or she is doing; whether or not he or she is happy with life in general; whether or not he or she is satisfied with his or her work and career; whether or not he or she is able to uphold a good balance between work, family and private life, and so on. By asking and answering these questions the employee becomes aware of his or her life and career and can begin to think about whether or not he or she is on the right track.

The second step is to establish a comprehensive "self analysis." Here, the employee is asked first to describe his or her personal characteristics, then to describe what he or she believes that other people would say are his or her main personal characteristics, and finally to point out which of these characteristics are his or her strong qualities and which are his or her weak qualities.

Based on this outline of the present situation in work and life and on the characterization of the personal self, the employee is, in the third step, given the task of working out his or her visions and goals, on the one hand concerning his or her work, and on the other hand, concerning the rest of his or her life. Once these steps are gone through, the coach helps the employee work out a concrete plan for how the career and life goals can be achieved. A behavioral therapist explained that "we make no difference here between work and life. Both are just as important and to make any improvements both areas need to be planned, strategic persons and issues need to be pointed out, etc." The life and career program takes about 4 to 6 weeks and is based on the principle that the knowledge and the information that is required to go through all the four steps should come from the individual participant. As said by the therapist:

> my role as a coach is to make the individual talk and reveal to him or herself what he or she really feels, thinks, and wants; if you will, it is this inner truth of the individual that I seek to bring forth. I will not say that one career is better than the other; that the individual should prioritize work or his or her family. I ask the questions and thereby direct the employees' attention in certain directions instead of others. But it is the individual who should come up with the answers. It is so much more powerful to hear yourself say what you feel about yourself, your job, etc., than to hear it from someone else.

Even though all these green programs are distinct on paper, in reality they seem to revolve around the same things. For instance, the BMI program seeks to help people eat 'healthier.' Yet, the basic purpose seems to be the same as all these other green activities and programs—to change people's mindset, to make them active and responsible for their individual performance at work, and even in life in general, thus ultimately being more able to work according to the self-managing principles of SPS. One employee who had recently participated in a health profile examination argued that

> previously I wasn't that concerned about my health and well-being, perhaps due to the fact that I am never sick. But now I know what can happen if you don't take preventive action. In these times when people are laid off due to the global financial crisis, you need to stay fit, and the health profile helps you to do so.

It has already been suggested that Scania's Health Organization (HO) has a mission to "act as a support for human development at Scania" as one senior manager put it. In addition to the aforementioned activities that aim to affect the employees to become healthier by becoming 'high-performing characters,' an ability to take initiative, of remaining motivated and, of course, of feeling well and satisfied with life in general, the HO unit is in charge of all canteens, where "a healthy diet that is set together by our dietary experts is served" as one of the managers of the HO unit explained. "Our ambition with this is first of all to offer our employees a healthy and nutritious breakfast and lunch; but also to inspire them to eat healthier at home." Further, the HO unit organizes regular championships at the workplaces where each employee gets a small apparatus that counts all the steps he or she takes during a week. Results are aggregated to the team level, where the team can win, for instance, a sweater, tickets to the cinemas or so on. One company nurse explained that these championships are very popular and have "increased the willingness to be active both at home and at work." A number of other championships are also organized, e.g. "lunch walks," where teams can win gifts if they take a walk after lunch using ski-sticks for at least 20 minutes. Further, in order to stress the importance of maintaining good health, when Scania celebrated its 100 years, a gift was given to all employees: a fitness center. The fitness center offers all employees and their families free of charge various fitness activities such as gym, tennis, badminton, squash, football, swimming, etc., all days of the week and is open between 6 a.m. and 11 p.m. One employee said that "after work you go there to meet colleagues, exercise a bit, eat at one of the restaurants, it's a nice environment where you can relax and feel at home." One of his colleagues stressed that

> Scania has always helped us to have an active leisure time, and the fitness centre is a great manifestation of this. It's good not only for those who don't have a family. During weekends families come here as well and enjoy each other's company. My daughter has got a lot of friends thanks to the fitness centre.

Under the regime of the fitness center, more than 35 "leisure activities" are organized that according to one of the managers of the HO unit "help improve our employees' well-being." These include arts clubs, football cups, painting, running, skiing, etc. One of the supervisors working at the fitness center explained that

> we want to help our employees to have a meaningful leisure time. This does not only include various activities, but also the promotion of meaningful relations between the employees. It's nice to see how many have become personal friends thanks to us. Breaking social isolation helps people stay fit and healthy, and in this way I think that the fitness centre and all we do helps our employees to improve their well-being.

Indeed, the fitness center is very popular among the employees according to internal surveys. One employee concluded that

> the fitness centre is part of my daily routine, and I would be very disappointed if they would close it down. It's the social thing that matters, you feel part of a family here and you feel proud to work for a company that gives so much support to its personnel.

8 Conclusion

A basic idea of this study is that investments in measures that aim to improve employees' health and well-being operate as principal means in the management of contemporary organizations. By drawing on our study of Scania, we will explore this managerial dimension of health promotion practices by distinguishing first, what the different policies, programs and activities devised by Scania's Health Organization (HO) focus on and seek to alter among those individuals whom they concern. That is, what type of problems induces these investments in the health and well-being of Scania's employees? Furthermore, what ethical substance are they trying to change or rectify in order to solve these problems and in order to improve the condition of the individual employees? Second, we discuss how the policies, programs and activities devised by the HO seek to achieve this 'improvement' of the condition of the individual employees. That is, through which methods and principles do the professionals at the HO try to alter specific aspects of individual employees' behavior, their physical and psychological conditions? Third, what kind of employee do these policies, programs and activities either implicitly or explicitly idealize? That is, what type of individual subject do the policies, programs and activities that the HO offers try to bring forth? In relation to that, what type of individual subject do they seek to prevent from surfacing? Finally, we wish to discern the underlying goals or visions that motivate this whole endeavor. That is, what does Scania intentionally or unintentionally achieve through the policies, programs and activities undertaken by the HO?

THE OBJECTS OF MANAGEMENT

With regard to the first issue, our study suggests that a common denominator of all activities and programs of the HO (regardless, if they are categorized as 'red,' 'yellow' or 'green'), is that they focus not just on employees' clinical conditions, but also on their daily routines. In itself there is, of course, nothing surprising about this; occupational health care has a long tradition in trying to determine the causal relations between employees' medical conditions and the environment in which the employees work. What may be interesting in our study, however, is first of all that many of the programs and activities that the HO offers, focus on employees' daily routines outside work. That is, many of those factors which are seen to explain or determine why an individual has become ill or injured, why an employee is or is not at risk of becoming ill or injured, and if an employee has the potential of improving his or her health, well-being, and professional performance, are sought in the overall lifestyles of the employees. It is there, it seems, in the ways and magnitudes that employees exercise, sleep, relate to their families and friends, eat, and so on, that much of what may turn out as future problems or future potentials are to be found. From a strictly technical and ergonomic perspective, the work environment should, of course, be safe. Employees should not risk getting hurt just because a machine system has sharp edges or is too hot. Furthermore, they should not end up with, for instance, back or knee problems just because the machines are ergonomically ill-designed. Yet, apart from such basic and restricted technical health issues, the health experts at the HO tend to understand the principles of organizing work (according to the SPS philosophy) as a second-order nature, i.e., as conditions that the HO can do little about; while, however, they regard the lifestyles of employees as potentially subject to their change management and purposeful organization. It is, in other words, the HO's main task to help the individual employees adapt to Scania's principles of production and organization, not the other way around.

Hence, employees' lifestyles are continually referred to as core factors in explaining employees' health, well-being and professional success. Still, judging by our study, employees' lifestyles are not by themselves the core ethical substance that the HO's activities and programs aim to change and improve. Since lifestyle changes cannot come from orders and directives, but only from employees' own free choices, it is not lifestyles per se, but that which is seen to lead employees toward freely choosing healthier lifestyles that the HO's activities and programs set as their main target. This target, it seems, is employees' motivation to constantly work on their abilities, trying to become healthier, more productive and more successful in life and work, thus exercising a kind of 'total leadership' (Friedman, 2006). A basic assumption of the HO's programs and activities is that the 'motivated employees' are less prone to become injured or ill, and they are considered more likely to improve their health, well-being and performance. Accordingly, the maintenance and furthering of a 'right type of motivation' is the fundamental task of the HO's health promotion activities and programs.

The significance and more precise meaning of this notion is expressed in the terms 'self-control,' 'self-discipline,' 'will power,' etc., which all point toward the personal qualities that are seen to be required to maintain health and well-being. Furthermore, these terms express that a 'right type of motivation' is an element of individuals who the HO can seek to define, maintain and promote; but that it cannot bring about if it is not already there. Motivation is in this regard the backbone of employees' moral character, a moral character that they are or are not gifted with. This is important to note, because it implies that the health promotion programs and activities are based on a subtle distinction between employees with and employees without an 'appropriate moral character.' Furthermore, it implies that the health promotion programs and activities are based on an assumption that health and well-being are ultimately a question of morals. Hence, to the same extent that those employees who display the 'right type of motivation,' or in other words, those employees who are strong in moral character, are seen as having the potential to develop their health, well-being, and professional abilities, the contrast theme is also implied: the fundamental reason why some employees lack potential to develop their health, well-being and professional abilities, relate to their 'lack of moral character.'

In claiming that the lifestyles, and more fundamentally, the motivation of employees to manage themselves, constitute the core ethical substances of the HO's programs and activities we are, however, not saying that the employees' lifestyles and motivation are the only or even the primary factors that the activities and programs that the HO offers seek to define, amend, change or alter. The HO's activities and programs still emphasize the importance of the physical working environment in explaining many of the bio-medical and psychological conditions of employees. In that regard the focus on employees' lifestyles and motivation can be seen as a complement to the traditional focus of occupational health care activities and programs. Yet, this complement is interesting and important because it is here, through these health promotion programs and activities that the domain of corporate jurisdiction is extended right into the private domains of employees' lives. This argument, however, implies two issues that the present study allows us to address. First, given that it has traditionally been part of the core practice of medical professionals to prescribe various treatments to their patients that will somehow interfere with the ways in which they live their lives, we need to distinguish in which specific cases we can say that the occupational health services accounted for in the present study represent a break with or an extension of traditional medical practices at workplaces. Furthermore, in direct connection to the first question, we need to distinguish on what grounds such an extension of the professional domain of occupational health care into the private sphere becomes legitimate. That is, if health-promoting activities among corporations have begun to regulate what employees do in their spare time, how they socialize with their families and friends and so on, how then is this enterprise motivated and legitimated as necessary and good acts that do not violate the privacy and integrity of individual subjects?

With regard to the first question, let us note that it has all along been part of the power that we associate with the medical profession to demand that a patient who has been diagnosed with some illness or injury obey the authority of the medical professional. In fact, this was what Parsons (1951), as has already been touched upon previously, meant by 'the sick role' in modern welfare states; provided that an individual who is diagnosed as sick or injured, subordinates to the authority of the medical doctor who has diagnosed the individual and who is about to treat him or her, the individual is released from some of the responsibilities of taking care of him or herself that all free and full citizens otherwise have to bear. A person with back problems who has been prescribed by his or her medical doctor to rest at home in bed must follow these instructions, otherwise the person may lose his or her rights to stay home from work and may be held responsible for the illnesses or injuries he or she has obtained. Hence, in this regard there is nothing spectacular about the fact that the corporate health experts of the HO unit give advice and instructions to the Scania employees that concern what they do in their private lives. However, our study also indicates how its programs and activities differ from these principles of the classical 'sick role.' First, the object of the HO's health promoting practices are not restricted in time and place to the changes in behavior of individuals deemed necessary by a medical professional to treat a particular medical issue; but concern permanent and general behavioral changes which are epitomized by the notion of the 'lifestyle' of the individual. Furthermore, especially when yellow or green programs and activities are concerned, these lifestyle changes suggested by the health authorities are not called for by an immediate and concrete health problem—be it in the form of some illness or injury— but by abstract, calculated health risks. This is then how the measures taken for the health and well-being of Scania's employees differ from traditional medical practices; rather than the classical sick role where a specific state of ill health establishes an authoritative relationship between a medical professional and an individual/patient, the health promoting practices at Scania revolve around a 'potential sick role' (Crawford, 1980). Rather than on diagnosed states of ill health, this 'potential sick role' is based on calculated health risks, which are related to the lifestyles and mindsets of the employees. Furthermore, rather than authoritative relationships and binding directives the 'potential sick role' establishes non-compelling and—seemingly— symmetrical relationships between health experts operating as coaches or counsellors and employees who are expected to freely make productive use of the advice they are thus given. Hence, on the one hand the health promotion practices of Scania reach further and are more ambitious than traditional medical practices. For they do not merely seek to subordinate the individual to temporary and restricted changes in behavior that are deemed necessary to become rehabilitated from a particular injury or illness; with the ambition of laying a foundation for general health and well-being they seek in addition to alter the ways of life that typically are seen to make up the identity of the individual. On the other hand, however, they are less authoritative. Rather than instructions that individuals are required to follow, they produce expert advice and moral guidance which are offered to employees as a form of service that they are expected to follow.

We have thus reached a point where we can answer the second question concerning the grounds upon which an extension of the professional domain of worksite health promotion into the private sphere of individuals' lives becomes legitimate. To some extent we have already begun answering this question because the earlier discussion points out that the health promotion practices at Scania circumvent the whole issue by being offered as opportunities that individuals choose rather than as directions that individuals are obliged to follow. That is, the 'professional gaze' of Scania's health experts legitimately penetrates into the private sphere of employees' lives because employees themselves freely choose to be coached or counselled in the art of lifestyle management; employees do not have to let the health experts know about their eating habits, about their leisure activities, family relations, and so on; instead they invite the health experts into their private world and they choose whether or not the expertise and moral guidance they provide are worth taking any notice of.

This notion, however, that the health services are merely offerings or opportunities that employees can choose or not choose to make use of to develop their health, well-being, and their careers, is problematic in two specific respects. On the one hand, we observed how the twin policies of 'employee-ship' and 'the 24 hour employee' point toward a flip side to this coin of free choice. For these policies continuously remind the employees of their responsibility for measuring up to the norms and ideals that make up the notion of 'the good Scania employee.' They signal that the good Scania employee is an individual who takes care of him or herself, who makes sure to eat right, who does not drink too much alcohol, who partakes in sports activities, etc. Overall, they suggest that the good Scania employee is an individual who sees work and private life as two spheres, which are separate, but productively linked, and where this link requires constant attention and purposeful organization. Hence, both these policies outline norms of 'good employee-ship' in relation to which the programs and activities that the HO offers comes forth as resources or opportunities that employees can—and should—make use of to adapt to these norms. Furthermore, these policies remind all line managers at Scania that they are expected to care for the employees during the work day as well as during the remainder of the day. That is, they signal that a line manager should pay attention to what his or her subordinates do after the working day has ended. Hence, the policies of 'employee-ship' and 'the 24 hour employee' make the subordinates' private lives a direct concern for line managers. Yet, as was underscored by several of them, in their role as managers they should be concerned about how their subordinates live their lives outside work, however, they should not interfere with this private sphere of their subordinates' lives. Just like Scania employees are implicitly referred back to the HO and its programs and activities when it comes to adapting to the norms of 'good employee-ship,' the line managers are referred back to these programs and activities in their attempts to shoulder the responsibilities for their '24 hour employees.' Hence, as a Scania employee you are free to disregard the life-style-oriented programs and activities that the HO offers, but if you fail to live up to the norms of 'good employee-ship' this can be held against you. As a line manager, as long as your subordinates are not ill or injured, you can choose both to disregard what employees do in their lives outside work and the lifestyle-oriented programs and activities that the HO offers. But if the employees end up ill, you can be blamed for not having lived up to the norms of 'the good Scania manager' who cares for his or her subordinates 24 hours a day.

On the other hand, the very concept of health that underlies Scania HO's programs and activities also seems to make the notion of free choice pro-blematic. Even though the different professionals and their associated pro-grams and activities differ somewhat in their view and handling of the concept of health, there is still a general tendency of making employees' lifestyles and motivation to improve in life and work, part of the definition of their health status. That is, the extent to which an employee is defined as healthy is not merely a matter of clinical diagnoses; it is also a matter of mapping the lifestyle of the employee and of determining the employee's level of motivation to work on him or herself to become healthier, more productive and able. Hence, an employee's motivation and lifestyle is not merely seen to determine employees' health; they are also seen as part of the very definition of whether or not the employee is healthy. This implies that an employee who for instance is defined via one of the HO's health screen-ings as not energetic or active enough, as lacking in motivation, and gen-erally as having a problematic lifestyle that is said to result in stress, poor working mates relations, etc., risks being regarded by the HO as 'unhealthy' and thereby as potentially sick. Furthermore, if it turns out that the observed lack of motivation and poor lifestyle of the employee make him or her unable to meet the performance criteria of work, the 'potentially sick role' may easily be transformed into a genuine 'sick role.' If this happens the medical professional at the HO can legitimately claim that it is for instance the weight problem and general physical incapacity that come from the assumed or declared 'passive lifestyle' and 'poor eating habits' that makes the employee unable to perform fully at work. Hence, in such a situation what is an offering of expertise and moral guidance toward a healthier life and a better career, becomes directives that the employee will have to follow to keep his or her job. Failure to comply with a medical rehabilitation plan may eventually lead to dismissal. It is in these respects, by the professional norms implied by the policies of 'employee-ship' and 'the 24 hour employee,' and by a concept of health that embraces the lifestyle and motivation of the employees, that the health promotion programs and activities offered by the HO come forth not merely as resources and oppor-tunities which are offered to the Scania employees, but also as implicit directives that employees must adhere to. It is furthermore in these respects that the programs and activities offered by the HO are not merely a form of care for the health and well-being of the Scania employees, but also is a specific form of managing employees' lifestyles and mindsets so that they conform to the criteria of the 'successful' Scania employee. It is to the principal functioning of this form of management that we now turn.

THE MANAGERIAL DIMENSIONS OF HEALTH PROMOTION

The policies of 'employee-ship' and the '24 hour employee' suggest how Scania's health promotion programs and activities establish a specific form of management, which operates by establishing norms of good and healthy conduct at work as well as in private life. The encompassing notion of health deployed by the HO in most of its programs and activities leads to a situation where those employees who break with the norms of 'good employee-ship' risk being considered unhealthy or ill. In these cases the HO's offerings of expertise and moral guidance, i.e., the offerings which employees have the formal right to disregard, are transformed into author-itative instructions that employees are obliged to follow. Being active and motivated when it comes to taking care of one's health risk is transformed into obligations and directives if one fails to meet the performance criteria of one's work. In short, the HO's programs and activities harbor both a *normative* and a—potentially—*coercive* form of control of the mindsets and lifestyles of Scania's employees. Both the normative and the coercive dimension of managerial control operate primarily on the 'exterior' of employees' subjectivities. That is, by indicating or prescribing what is appropriate and/or required behavior of the employees these programs and activities indirectly or directly limit employees' autonomy to live and to work in other ways. However, these programs and activities also harbor a third dimension of managerial control, which is distinguished from the other two in that it does not set limits to individuals' freedom to act differently, but seeps into the identities of individuals. From this perspective, the health promotion programs and activities operate as instruments of managerial power by affecting how employees deploy their freedom; that is, they oper-ate not as instruments that directly or indirectly control employees' behavior, but as instruments that 'make up' individuals' social identities.

In this sense, health promotion programs and activities can be understood as expansions of the type of control that organization sociologists have explored in contemporary human resource management (HRM) techniques that aim to bring out a kind of 'positive leadership' of oneself by remaining committed and active (e.g. Barratt, 2002; Covaleski *et al.*, 1998; Townley, 1994). The idea is then that HRM becomes an instrument and ideology of power, not by forcing directives onto employees, but by accumulating knowledge about employees—their attitudes, competencies, desires, etc.—and by using this knowledge to direct and control employees more delicately and unobtrusively; in ways which are aligned with their 'true' faculties and interests. HRM techniques such as yearly development talks, attitude surveys, mentoring programs, etc. are seen to operate as instruments that 'help' employees freely adapt their professional identities to the values and principles of work. In a similar yet extended vein, health promotion programs and activities operate as power/knowledge instruments that 'help' employees adjust their subjectivities so that the choices they freely make at work as well as in their private lives become aligned with the values and principles that lead the organization toward its goals. The significance of founding this form of control of employees on knowledge and expertise appear to be even stronger than in the case of HRM techniques. By preventing forms of control that focus on individuals' selves and lifestyles to become offensive and intrusive, they must be exercised indirectly by way of the distance and legitimacy provided by knowledge and expertise (Rose, 1999). The health promotion expertise of the HO at Scania establish that necessary distance between the individual employee and the power of the organization. For instance, employees' problems of coping with their work at Scania were sometimes seen to be related to some personal or family-related matter. Yet, in these cases the supervisors and line managers find it inappropriate for them to interfere, first, because their area of jurisdiction as managers concern work, not employees' private lives, and second, because they do not want to make the manager–employee relationship too 'personal' and 'close.' In these cases, the managers can turn to the HO and its professionals to deal with 'delicate matters,' because health experts are entitled to have a say about people's private concerns that line managers should not interfere with. Hence, the health experts can make use of its expertise and its legitimate position to help employees lead 'better lives' for their own good but also for Scania's development.

At a basic level, health promotion programs and activities are provided to employees in the name of people's health and well-being, and are handled by 'independent' and legitimate health professionals, that tend to obscure the forces of managerial control in them; making them seem merely as informed ways of helping employees lead 'healthier' and 'more successful' lives. And to some extent that is precisely what they are and what they do: they provide expertise and moral guidance as to how specific individuals can help themselves become better and more productive Scania employees—24 hours a day. In this respect the type of managerial control exercised via the health promotion programs and activities is not repressive and restrictive, but supportive; it empowers individuals in making themselves up as particular types of subjects who are at once geared toward good health and professional development. It is this combination of care and control that appear to make them such subtle instruments of power. At a more specific level, the subtle form of control that the health promotion programs and activities make possible comes from the way in which they combine the two principally—but not practically—distinct power/knowledge regimes that Foucault (1997) termed "disciplinary power" and "pastoral power." Disciplinary power is exercised through knowledge generated through examinations of individuals, whereas pastoral power is exercised via knowledge that comes from individual confessions. Both disciplinary power and pastoral power are based on knowledge and expertise. Yet, whereas the expert in disciplinary power is a 'neutral' observer who makes use of scientific methods to monitor, document and analyze the objective characteristics of the 'patient,' the expert in pastoral power is a counsellor who makes use of the patients' avowals of his or her own subjective truth to provide moral guidance.

Several of the programs and activities that the HO at Scania offers the employees are good examples of disciplinary power/knowledge. The health screenings, the health dialogue service, the BMI program, the health talks, etc. all exemplify programs and activities that discipline employees via detailed examinations of the employees' lifestyles, family situations, work habits, stress reactions and so on. These examinations constitute the employees as objects of knowledge that can be categorized, compared and advised by the corporate health experts more discretely, intimately and possibly, with less conflict and friction. The employees become known and categorized as employees who are physically active or inactive, as healthy or unhealthy eaters, as overweight, normal or too slim, as motivated to improve their health, etc.

After having passed through these programs and activities, the employees become known to the HO and to Scania in a far more detailed and personal sense than could be provided by any traditional HRM program; for whereas HRM programs and HRM experts focus on work- related issues, these health promotion programs and activities legitimately open up the private lives of employees to the scrutinizing gaze of experts who seek to help individuals become good '24 hour employees.' The multi-professional teams of the HO play a central role here. As recalled, the teams are seen to constitute what the managers of the HO referred to as "core knowledge centres"; sites where different yet complementary lines of expertise are brought into play to accumulate knowledge, which, as suggested by one manager, was used to make sure both that the employees are healthy and motivated and that Scania is utilizing its human resources as effectively as possible. Overall, the form of discipline that is exercised by the teams open up possibilities for the HO to transcend a reactive stance toward the employees. The knowledge base that the teams generate through their practice and that is analyzed by the HO's statisticians, does not only help to make HO a legitimate authority in the reactive management of Scania employees' concrete health problems—momentary illnesses, accidents, physical deficiencies, etc. Rather, by generating generalized knowledge about Scania's employees, the HO can take initiatives and act on risks related to accidents that have not yet occurred, or on potential gains in motivation, in physical or psychological well-being, which are yet to be realized.

This ability of taking proactive initiatives directed toward potential health hazards or potential gains in health and well-being is very important for the strategic influence of the HO within Scania. On the one hand, the HO can legitimately claim to have a say about decisions regarding the organization of work and the management of the employees without there being any concrete health problem that needs to be taken care of. Differently put, rather than having to deal with issues and problems that follow from strategic decisions regarding the future management and organization of Scania, the HO can legitimately claim to be part of these decisions. On the other hand, however, it drastically expands the clientele that the HO can address and legitimately influence. For instance, through the statistics gathered by the HO on all employees' health and well-being, the organization develops a general and 'statistically certified' (almost scientifically legitimate) knowledge about the employees and about how different ways of organizing work affects the health and efficiency of Scania's employees. As a result, the HO can then use its expertise to suggest changes which concern not only those who are ill or injured but the rest of the personnel as well. Hence, the wealth of knowledge generated by the teams open up possibilities for the HO and for Scania to legitimately act on and interfere with the working life and the private lives of all Scania employees, including that of its top management team.

It is not merely the case that the HO, as a result of the knowledge accumulated by the multi-professional teams, can legitimately guide employees in the art of lifestyle management. It is also the case that the disciplinary gaze of its various health professionals and their different programs and activities 'seep' into the very identities of the employees, making them up as particular types of subjects that either fit in at Scania or not. For instance, people who go through the programs of the so-called Health School know that they have been given a chance to learn more about themselves. Obviously, it is they themselves who have to decide upon their careers and their private lives. But to do that they need to know who they are and what their specific personal characteristics make them suitable for. They also need to know how they can change and 'improve' themselves. If nothing else, that is what the Health School tries to help them accomplish. By going through all these programs and tests and by discussing the results, they potentially come to know more about themselves. The disciplinary gaze does not merely operate 'on the exterior' of individuals, limiting and directing individuals' courses of action. Individuals' desire to understand who they are, coupled with their awareness of potentially being under observation, tend to lead them to gradually internalize the disciplinary gaze so that they slowly become their own masters and servants, thus taking command of and leading all aspects of their lives. More specifically, the examinations of the health screenings, the Health School, the health talks, the health dialogue service, etc. as offered by Scania's HO have the potential to discipline (exercise power via knowledge and expertise) the employees from the *outside in*. That is, 'objective and legit-imate knowledge' about employees' lifestyles, about their eating habits, family relations, etc., are attributed to the employees who become 'subjectified' by gradually internalizing this knowledge, letting it define their identities.

However, in most of the health promotion programs and activities the examining part appears merely as a foundation or point of departure for the more significant confessional/therapeutic part. In contrast to the examina-tion part, the confessional/therapeutic part of the health promotion pro-grams and activities incite a form of control that operate on the individual employee from the *inside out*; i.e., it encourages the employee to declare, "reflect on and analyze his or her own thoughts and conduct, under the watchful gaze of an authoritative figure, and to correct or to reform him or herself" (Barratt, 2002: 192). Through the interviews, therapy and counsel-ling that are part of all the different health promotion programs and activ-ities at Scania, the employees are encouraged to avow their "inner truth" to the health professional at the HO, making it available for interpretation and careful advice as to how the employees should work on themselves in order to become more efficient and productive Scania employees. It appears to be in this form that the health promotion programs and activities have the potential of operating most delicately as mechanisms of managerial control at Scania. The knowledge about employees' lifestyles, professional ambi-tions, problems, social relations, etc. does not ultimately come from an external observer, but from the employees themselves. The health profes-sionals at the HO are seen merely to translate or interpret that inner truth of employees into what employees found to be a 'better understanding of who they are' and possibly, of what they might become. Hence, whereas the disciplinary examinations of the employees lead to their 'subjectification' (cf. Townley, 1994), the confessional dimension of the health promotion programs and activities constitute a pastoral form of power which lead to employees' 'self-subjectification.' That is, the employees do not only subject themselves to the objectified image of their selves that various examination techniques have generated; by confessing and declaring their wants, needs, attitudes and despairs to a health coach, a therapist, diet expert, etc., the employees are also helped to make themselves up as particular selves by the "objectification of the self by the self" (Foucault, 1980: 240).

In all, how should we understand the forms of control that we outline here? Should we see them as examples of a more subtle, extended, obscure, intimate and totalitarian control? Or should we in fact see them as enabling individuals to develop and to liberate their full potentials? In trying to answer this question, let us look at an interesting parallel between the notion of 'self-subjectification' and the notion of 'strategized subordination,' developed by, e.g. Burawoy (1979) and Deetz (1998). Their usage of this notion is interesting in that it can be seen to epitomize organization sociologists' way of judging contemporary forms of organizational control such as HRM and organizational culture. 'Strategized subordination' is then used to discuss forms of control where employees become accomplices in their own exploitation. In Deetz's (1998) study of management consulting firms, it is for instance argued how employees tend not merely to passively consent to managerial control, but actively embrace it by striving to achieve the identity as consultants that top management has articulated for them. That is, the desire of earning an identity as a fully-fledged consultant is exploited by top management as a way of driving employees to strategize their selves so that they work harder, better and longer. Deetz claims that the price the employees have to pay for this strategizing of their selves often is ill health, social and family unrest, and so on. That is, the employees actively embrace a subjectivity which leads them to overemphasize the significance of their professional lives and to neglect their private lives.

The similarity between the ideas that are contained in the notion of 'strategized subordination' and what we refer to as 'self-subjectification' is fairly obvious; both terms refer to employees' active subordination to a particular type of identity and style of work/life. The differences, however, are more significant: for whereas 'strategized subordination' is driven by the abstract and status overloaded image of the good employee that management has articulated, 'self-subjectification' is driven by the intimate truth about the self that the individual him- or herself has declared. Furthermore, whereas the 'strategized subordination' that results from the desire to earn a particular professional identity implies the suppression of conflicts between this identity and other identities associated with private life, the 'self-subjectification' that results from health promotion programs and activities, implies that private life is treated as part of the compound totality that requires disciplined attention and self-managed control. In this respect, health promotion and the 'self-subjectification' processes that it gives rise to can be seen as functionally linked to the kind of work/life problems that 'strategized subordination' among many occupational groups in contemporary working life tends to generate. In these processes of 'self-subjectification,' the health expert not only functions as a translator of the inner truth of the employee, he or she is also a moral guide, i.e., an authoritative figure who makes use of this inner truth for the sake of helping the employee adjust his or her self and lifestyle to the criteria of health and professional success (Conrad, 1994).

So, what is our answer to the questions raised earlier? We are bound to answer both 'yes' and 'no.' On the one hand, the health promotion programs and activities that we have studied do not lure employees to actively repress those parts of their selves and their lives that do not comply with norms of professional success created by top management (cf. Burawoy, 1979; Deetz, 1998; Kunda, 1992; Willmott, 1993). On the contrary, they empower employees in their attempts to fashion all aspects of their selves in accord with criteria of health, well-being and professional success. On the other hand, however, it is precisely in this regard that the health promotion programs and activities become more truly totalitarian than those

HRM techniques and organizational culture programs that organization sociologists have often studied. They promote employees in their attempts to strategize not only their professional selves and professional lives, but their entire selves and lives. Hence, it is not only the work but also the life of the employee that should be strategically managed. The employee is given the 'freedom' and 'responsibility' to do so. As observed in our study of Scania, the 'good employee' is a subject that manages him- or herself 24 hours a day.

MAKING UP THE HEALTHY EMPLOYEE

Up until this point, we have sought to explicate how the health promotion programs and activities at Scania come to operate as instruments that control employees by disciplining and counselling them to freely adopt particular subjectivities. Let us now turn to the content of these subjectivities. Differently put, let us now turn toward the question of what type of individual subjectivities the health promotion programs and activities idealize and what type of individual subjectivities they implicitly scorn. To some extent we have already addressed this issue, since the employee that these programs and activities implicitly idealize is a direct reflection of some fundamental ethical substances that the health promotion programs and activities of the HO seek to address, correct and promote. Salient among these is the notion of the employee who is *aware*, not only about health issues, but about all things that can either endanger or promote his or her life and work. More fundamentally, the healthy employee is *self-aware*; i.e., he or she possesses self-knowledge about the impulses, faculties and shortcomings that are associated with his or her specific personality and lifestyle. According to Scania's fundamental values, in today's world employees have to be able to take care of themselves. Scania can try to motivate people and teach them about healthy lifestyles, about healthy eating, about stress, and so on. But ultimately, what will prove to be most important is whether or not Scania can help them understand themselves better. Nothing is as important as this. To take good care of yourself, people have to maintain some kind of relation to themselves and they have to know what works for them and what does not. If Scania can help them with that, then it has contributed to their 'progress' as individuals and as employees.

These notions of awareness and self awareness require employees who are mindful and responsible and who make disciplined decisions about work and private life. They point in the direction of a conscious and thinking individual who does not merely give in to impulses and habits, but considers alternatives and make choices among them that comply with what is good in the long run. Put differently, they point in the direction of a rational individual who subordinates all parts of his or her life to principles of self-management. Yet, the kind of employee who is idealized by the health promotion programs and activities is not only a reflective being, but also an *active, energetic,* and *positive* being. The healthy individual does not passively wait for directives and instructions from others; the healthy individual is a 'doer,' a person who takes on work and private life with a positive, pragmatic and flexible attitude, always seeking opportunities to improve the current state of affairs. Not only is activity and a positive attitude seen to lead to health and well-being, but they are also seen as a direct expression of health and well-being. Together, these characteristics—being aware, self-aware, active, positive and responsible—imply a crucial and delicate balance between stepping aside, sensibly reflecting on the work/life situation as such and taking action. Maintaining this balance is a matter of management, or more precisely, it is a matter of self-management, of being able to control all aspects of one's life. This, it seems, is the most important and fundamental task of the health promotion programs and activities of Scania's HO: to counsel employees into adopting the particular mindset required to achieve this self-management. The healthy Scania employee continuously alternates between doing and reflecting. Hence, this employee is both a 'doer' and a 'thinker.' It is a person who actively and flexibly approaches all parts of his or her life strategically, attempting to manage them purposefully.

This mindset is an almost exact match of the principles of the Scania Production System (SPS). As recalled, the introduction of the SPS was motivated by the poor production quality, the lack of productivity and the high personnel turnover rates of the old Tayloristic factory regime. The introduction of the SPS had been a drawn out and problem-ridden process, not because it was ill-conceived, but because it opened up a need for a new type of factory worker. This new ideal worker was an altogether different being from the obedient, non-thinking servant required by the old Tayloristic regime. It was an active, thinking and social being who perceived his or her work as a matter of dynamically contributing to a team, whose responsibility it was to alternate between following the principles and rules of the SPS and trying to conceive of ways to further improve the SPS. That is, the new ideal worker is in many ways a direct reflection of the healthy individual that the programs and activities of the HO seek to bring forth, which is concretely done by detecting behavioral deviances (framed as existing or potential health problems) that should be corrected along the ideas of 'constant improvement.' Of course, it is not the case that Scania established and expanded the HO with all its different professionals, programs and activities with the explicit purpose of fashioning a new worker fit for the new SPS factory regime. That is, we are not suggesting that the sophisticated system established by the HO that ties together the health and well-being of the employees with the economy of the factory would have been the result of a rational and cunning plan. On the contrary, the full-scale operation of the HO may have been the result of a step-by-step process initially driven by the partly divergent interests of the unions at Scania and Scania's managerial headquarters. As recalled, the SPS was explained to be a synthesis of a dialectical process between the management of Scania, that wished to see SPS as a system that would increase production efficiency, and the unions that wished to see SPS as a system that would replace inhuman Tayloristic production principles with more humane production principles. In the midst of this struggle, around the mid-1990s, the expansion of the HO appears to have been a political instrument in the attempts of corporate headquarters to win the unions' approval of the SPS. That 'the mindset of the worker' at Scania was one of the major hurdles in the implementation of the SPS regime was not apparent at the outset. Yet, even though it might have been the result of a partly unintentional process, it was during this phase the principles of health and well-being joined forces with the principles of efficient production. In the name of health and well-being, the HO has come to function as a human resource management function that reaches further and deeper into the lives and identities of Scania's employees than any regular HRM department ever can. With the SPS, the same principles that are seen to lead toward a healthier and more rewarding life are now seen to lead to more efficient work and to better careers. In this situation, the health professionals of the HO have gradually become a specific group of managers of Scania; only they have the professional competence and the legitimacy of fully managing employees' lives and selves as corporate resources.

In all, the potentials of a health-promoting management regime are fairly obvious, which can explain their general success in the world of corporations and other organizations. It promises to replace traditional management techniques that subordinate employees to authoritative rules and regulations with concomitant negative consequences for their health and well-being; with management techniques that operate through employees' willingness to subordinate to their own ambitions of self-improvement. By working on oneself to stay healthy both at work and at home, there is in this way the potential for reducing absence due to sickness and injuries. Hence, worksite health promotion has a potential of health enhancement among employees, and overall cost containment for employers. One of the most interesting potentials of worksite health promotion from a corporate point of view, however, is the molding of an organizational culture that rewards activity and commitment. A 'healthy organization' encourages employees and managers to make 'healthy choices' and to behave in a health-promoting manner that may fundamentally affect organizational morale and productivity. As already said, in the case of Scania, the worksite health promotion that is core to the HO's activities are closely related to how the company's production system (SPS) functions and develops, which is a system that is regarded to be one key factor of Scania's economic success and performance for at least the years 1999–2009. The health experts of the HO unit play an important role as managers in enacting this enterprise. In this way, corporate health professionals are not only medical experts concerned with rather narrow problems of individual health and well-being; they are rather concerned, albeit in a latent and unobtrusive way, with the strategic management of corporations and other work organizations.

However, no matter how benevolent its ambitions may be, this management regime is essentially still a set of principles of exercising power, and power, as Foucault (1980) has stated, is neither good nor bad, but always potentially dangerous. This study stresses several pitfalls with a health-promoting management regime. One of these relates to how it contributes to establishing a new form of work ethic that challenges the boundary that has traditionally been drawn between work and private life. By crossing this boundary it does not dissolve or make the distinction between work and private life less important. On the contrary, it tends to make it more important not the least since stress, burnout and other health issues are typically seen to be related to a failure to maintain a proper balance and distinction between work and private life. Yet, it contributes to making management not merely a question of work, but of life in a more general sense. It is the life of the individual who should be managed, it is the work/life distinction that should be organized, and it is the individual him or herself who should handle this organization of 'the life puzzle' for the sake of remaining not only healthy and satisfied, but also employable and productive. Hence, this new work ethic opens for a new allocation of responsibilities; for as the causes of health problems are no longer primarily sought and found at work, but in the lifestyles of employees, the responsibility for managing these risks tends to be transferred from employers to employees. Whereas the employers' responsibility becomes limited to that of providing employees with opportunities, e.g. in the form of health promotion programs and activities, the employees' responsibility is extended so that 'healthy lifestyles' become part of the work/life capabilities that they are expected to nurture.

Overall, our observations suggest that the central capability in the quest for better health, well-being and professional success is self-management. The main task of health experts is to provide employees with the proper knowledge and skills to exercise self-discipline so that they can sensibly steer free from various health risks such as stress, burnout, fatigue and various physical problems. In itself, this seems to be an important enterprise. Yet, in the process of providing employees with the knowledge and power they require to manage themselves, the view that employees risk being struck by ill health may be transformed into the view that employees put themselves at risk of ill health. That is, the employee who suffers from ill health may seem to have 'chosen' improper food, to have neglected exercise, to have failed to maintain a fruitful and healthy balance between work and private life, and so on. Rather than having been struck by ill health, such an employee has failed to make proper use of the knowledge and skills provided by the health promoting programs. Furthermore, once this transformation has occurred, those who have failed in choosing a path that leads to health, well-being and professional success may not only be seen as failures, but also as sinners. To the extent that their failure to exercise self-discipline results in someone else having to do their work, "those who are deemed 'at risk' become the sinners, not the sinned against, because of their apparent voluntary courting of risk" (Lupton, 1995: 90). Such people may be stigmatized in society as irrational, self-deluding and irresponsible; because their neglect to control health risks becomes a form of evidence of a lack of potential of managing themselves.

9   Social and Political Implications

A critical idea in this book is that worksite health promotion (WHP) is an important mechanism for the successful accomplishment of modern management principles that favor responsibility, commitment and activity. In the previous chapter we argued that the positive side of this enterprise is the empowering of people who are willing and able to work hard and with much dedication. The negative side is its potential of making more transparent those that do not meet the requirements of the present system. That is, health promotion risks breeding intolerance for signs of 'weakness' or 'deviance.' Furthermore, the health promotion discourse's emphasis on individual responsibility may also breed a tendency of treating individuals' 'failures' as self-inflicted, the result of the individual's own choices, behaviors, and attitudes. The 'problematic' individuals are seen to be responsible for 'not having done enough,' or for just having behaved incorrectly; i.e. for provocatively deviating from norms and codes of 'healthy and employable behavior.' Hence, in contemporary society 'unhealthy' individuals, constructed as such through modern principles of health promotion (primarily at the workplace but also in other settings), risk eventually ending up as unemployable. In order to become employable again, these people need to undergo a social transformation which involves not only the learning of certain technical skills, but also the adoption of a lifestyle and sets of personal characteristics that make them come forth as 'healthy.' In this way measures that are taken in order to promote the health of employees may become constitutive parts of what are considered as 'good' and 'promising' employees. That is, the healthy employee is seen as the good employee; an increasing number of those individuals that are unwanted by contemporary labor markets are regarded as sick or disabled.

As already said, the concern for employees' health that we witness today is by itself not a new phenomenon. It has held a central position in political and economic discourses throughout most of the twentieth century. Furthermore, many of those welfare institutions that were formed since the 1940s—public health care, public schools and child care, etc., were more or less directly related to an interest in maintaining a workforce that was healthy and fit to function as employees (Downie et al., 1996). Yet, in the transformation of the traditional welfare regimes that have taken place during the last decades, the forms of health expertise, the relations between health experts and individuals, and the very notion of health has changed in the direction of health promotion. Even so, the magnitude of these changes should not be exaggerated. In contemporary societies, where production for profit remains the organizing principle of the economy, the concern for employees' health continues to be a part of a more general concern with securing some kind of correspondence between the principles of producing and selling commodities at a profit and the sets of implicit and explicit rules and norms that govern individual and collective conduct. A stable system for the allocation of a net product between consumption and production implies a corresponding system for the maintenance and reproduction of a population of individuals capable and willing to act as producers, be it in the form of employees, entrepreneurs, self-employed persons or consumers. To be legitimate and successful, any initiative or struggle aimed at improving the competitiveness of a company or a nation will have to be adapted to or find a way of adapting the body of norms, values, laws, infrastructure, etc. that govern individuals' conduct. Conversely, any attempt to improve the health and well-being of a company's personnel or a nation's population will have to consider its effects on the population's abilities and willingness to adapt to criteria of production and consumption.

Hence, political and economic debates and struggles between classes, interest groups, etc. will either directly or indirectly revolve around this relation between the capitalist system's specific principles of accumulating profit and the modes and doctrines of governing populations and individuals. Given that a capitalist system is unstable and thus liable to undergo successive transformations, the concern for and the attempts at securing the correspondence between the economy and the lives of individuals and populations will inescapably be tentative. It is well- known that a capitalist system is crisis-prone because of its paradoxical tendency of requiring considerable stability to function while constantly setting in motion destabilizing forces. Its inherent instability then derives from its inescapable growth orientation (crisis is defined as a lack of growth, so it must constantly grow and change); from that growth is pursued in more or less unpredictable competition between corporations; and from that growth in real values rests on the more or less unpredictable control and subordination of living labor to the principles of capitalist production and consumption (cf. Aglietta, 1979; Harvey, 1982).

Given these destabilizing forces, the overall problem throughout the history of capitalist societies has been to "bring the behaviors of all kinds of individuals—capitalists, workers, state employees, financiers, and all manner of other political-economic agents—into some kind of configuration that will keep the regime of accumulation functioning" (Harvey, 1989: 121). Our interest in the maintenance and control of the health of the working population is more restricted in that it primarily concerns the general problem in industrial societies to maintain and convert men and women's capacity to do work into labor processes that generate profit. What's more, the subordination and control of the working population to principles of production and consumption obviously involves a multitude of different activities—education, the mobilization of social sentiments (loyalty, professional pride, etc.), emotional identifications created via the media, etc., out of which the measures directly and indirectly taken in the names of individuals' health constitute but a small part. Nevertheless, these measures are important to study because they tend to concern much broader issues than those of maintaining a working population that is 'fit' for work in a strictly clinical sense. More specifically, over and above that of securing individuals' physical and psychological fitness for work, measures taken in the name of the health of employees tend to play a part in the socialization of employees who lead lives which correspond to moral criteria of what is considered 'a good life' and 'a good person.'

However, what can be more beneficial than promoting good health and reducing sickness and disability? In adopting and carrying out various strategies of health promotion, societies and organizations are seen as acting in the interests of their members, seeking to improve their health and contributing to the overall morale and culture. According to Lupton,

> in its reliance upon scientific expertises and emphasis on neutrality, public health discourse conforms to other social policy governmental activities of capitalist states, which are founded on the notion of the neutral and beneficent state acting in the best interests of the majority and standing above vested interests.
>
> (1995: 61)

Lupton noted, however, that the discourse on health promotion has not escaped criticism, neither by politicians, nor by scholars. From the political right-wing it has typically been criticized for functioning as a mechanism of an overly authoritarian state. From this perspective, health promotion is seen to convey risks of restricting individual freedom if they become part of the state's programs and techniques for governing populations. From a political left-wing position, a critique has been developed which also centers on the value of individual freedom. It is then the authoritarian and patronizing tenor of health promotion rhetoric that is addressed. Health promotion is seen to be open for victim blaming in that it individualizes responsibility for health by neglecting to consider the macrostructural causes of ill health (Crawford, 1980; Lupton, 1995).

Such political debates extend as well into the academic conversation on health promotion. As suggested by Thorogood, a sociology of health promotion should not ask what sociological analysis can contribute to the increased effectiveness of health promotion, but *what* is the role of health promotion and can it be uncritically regarded as 'good'? Sociological enquiry can reveal the norms and values that underpin health promotion; it might also ask questions about the nature of health promotion as a discourse.

(1992: 66)

In a review of the literature, Nettleton and Bunton (1995: 42) proposed the common distinction in medical sociology between, on the one hand, literature *of* health promotion, and, on the other hand, literature *for* health promotion. The latter seeks to refine and develop the techniques and practices of health promotion; the former pursues critical analyses of the underlying assumptions inherent in health promotion itself. This distinction is useful in that it implies that there is one literature that maintains a restricted focus on normative and prescriptive health issues, and another literature that seeks to describe and understand health promotion more generally as a set of ideas and practices which are imbued with certain (class) interests.

More specifically, there are two main sources of critique of health promotion that this study aims to extends. One is a 'structural critique,' which basically argues that health promotion has the potential for the victim blaming tendencies that was addressed earlier by not taking into account the material disadvantages of people's lives set both by limitations in the physical and mental constitution as in the economic, cultural and social environment. In this respect health promotion has the potential to act as a mechanism for deviance amplification and can reinforce the stigma associated with sickness and unhealthiness. It can, for example, serve to project an image of disablement as personal tragedy rather than as a socially produced state. This critique stresses that health promotion largely ignores the consequences of industrial capitalism such as social inequalities, poverty and pollution. Blaxter (1990: 5) argued that "in the context of health, choices about food, about smoking and drinking, and about the way in which leisure time is spent, are often thought to be most relevant," i.e. people manage themselves and their lives. But there are also persistent socioeconomic influences upon health: income, work, housing, and the physical and social environments that are part of one's way of living. Hence, should health promotion policies primarily be individualistic, thus placing responsibility on the individual, or should they rather be collectivistic?

Nettleton and Bunton (1995: 45) argued that on the one hand many of the most important diseases at present are 'self-inflicted'; but on the other hand, this approach minimizes the social and economic factors which are outside the individual's control. In the health promotion discourse, the self that is being constructed is that of an enterprising and entrepreneurial self, an individual who is interested in and willing to take action to improve his or her way of living and acting. It is assumed that all individuals have the potential for such social action in the name of good health, and that it is simply up to the health promotion officer to encourage or 'facilitate' the realization of this potential. Hence, the discourse assumes a 'free subject' who has a number of "choices of action" (Lupton, 1995: 61). However, as already suggested, definitions of 'healthy' and 'normal' are not fixed and 'choice' is not equally available to all people and choices are themselves circumscribed by material conditions. The individualizing tendencies of health promotion come from its focus on people's lifestyles as the primary determinant of their health.

Typically to the extent that a 'structural analysis' of health promotion is conducted, the focus is on the individual as the primary unit of analysis: health promotion supposes making the *healthy* choice to be the most important. It therefore assumes that this is also how any rational person would act. "The task for health promotion is then to remove obstacles, both individual and social structural, to this choice" (Thorogood, 1992: 73). Hence, the health promotion discourse maintains that 'good health' is the responsibility of the individual. It tends to individualize health and ill health states, removing them from the broader social context. However, regarding corporate initiatives to promote employees' health there is, as Polanyi *et al.* (2000: 146) put it, "the danger that a focus on individual lifestyles is simply a self-serving effort by competitive companies to reduce health care benefits costs as much as possible, without addressing deeper, job-related and organizational factors influencing health." Similarly, Rose (2001: 6–7) has argued in his analysis of public health projects pursued by various nations that "the state tries to free itself of some of the responsibilities that it acquired across the 20th century for securing individuals against the consequences of illness and accident," thus enhancing the obligations that individuals and families have for monitoring and managing their own health, where every citizen becomes an active partner in the drive for health, accepting responsibility for securing their own well-being. According to this paradigm, health promotion consists in a variety of strategies that try to identify, treat, manage or administer those individuals, groups or localities where risk is seen to be high.

Certainly the health promotion discourse has acknowledged that health problems may originate outside the individual, "but since these problems are also behavioral, solutions are seen to lie within the realm of individual choice" (Crawford, 1980: 365). In the case of worksite health promotion, critics have argued that the "lifestyle discourse may serve managerial interests by obscuring workplace-generated disease" (Zoller, 2003: 178). Concerns about environmental health threats may not disappear from managers' agenda as a result of health promotion activities. However, as suggested by our own study, attention is probably shifted to lifestyle hazards and individual solutions. Crawford (1980) argued that as political language, individual responsibility is highly problematic since it promotes a conception which overlooks the social constraints against 'choosing' in the sense elaborated previously. In this way there is a tendency in society to expand the definition of illness and disease to include a wide range of social phenomena. That is, people suffering from this expanded range of disease and illness states are increasingly evaluated in psychological or moral terms. This leads to a situation where people are seen to become ill because they deserve to; simply put, they are held up to blame for their unhealthy lifestyle. In this connection, when health and illness are seen to be moral concepts the classical Parsonian sick role that was discussed earlier cannot suffice as an adequate explanation when analyzing health and disease as moral concepts. 'Healthism,' however, focuses on what we can do for ourselves as individuals, blame is brought front-stage. In other words, the no-fault principle contained in the classical sick role formulation is replaced by a 'your fault' dogma. In this sense the relevance of the notion of a

> *potential-sick role* through which the obligation to stay healthy is more strongly asserted. In the potential-sick role, societal expectations are imposed on behalf of prevention. As potentially sick, individuals are experiencing more intense social pressures to act in ways to minimize that potential.
>
> (Crawford, 1980: 379)

To repeat, the ideology of individual responsibility promotes a concept of wise living. Potentially, it obscures the social forces that influence well-being, trying to solve 'the problem' in the individual, not the society. "Contrary to claims and first impressions, the new health consciousness (in its healthiest manifestations) entails a further medicalization of our culture, and, in particular, a medicalization of how the problem of health is understood" (Crawford, 1980: 369), where all the more 'deviant' behavior is defined in terms of sickness, and 'normalcy' in terms of health. In this sense the concept of 'medicalization' can be understood as having two broad meanings: one is the linking of an increasing range of social phenomena with the institution of medicine, e.g. the profession of medicine, therapeutic practice and medical diagnosis. In this usage, medicalization is usually described as an expansion of professional power over wider spheres of life, especially deviant behaviors. The other meaning of medicalization is the extension of the range of social phenomena mediated by the concepts of health and illness. Certainly,

> encouraging individuals to engage in preventive health activities possibly avoids one form of 'medicalization' (clinical). On the other hand, it takes up another form (preventive medicine and 'self-care') that moves medical and health concerns into every corner of everyday life.
>
> (Lupton, 1997: 107)

The other source of criticism of health promotion that the present study aims to extend is the so-called 'surveillance critique' (Nettleton and Bunton, 1995). It designates those studies that have focused on the programs and technologies of health promotion and how these serve, on the one hand, to monitor and regulate populations, and, on the other hand, to construct new identities. For instance, Bunton (1992: 4) argued that "health promotion is not only a new form of health care provision but also a new form of social regulation and control." Techniques for monitoring and evaluating people's 'health' are then seen to focus attention on increasingly detailed aspects of everyday life. A concern for 'positive health' takes health promotion specialists into previously unmonitored aspects of people's lives. Techniques for monitoring and evaluating people's 'health' focus attention on increasingly detailed aspects of everyday life. Health promotion programs introduce forms of social control that are not ostensibly oppressive nor obviously controlling, which is a central idea to the modern management principles that have been the subject of interest in this study. In these, often innocuous-looking forms they nevertheless enter and regulate individuals' lives in new ways. With regard to this notion of extended and more intimate surveillance, there may be important difficulties for employees to resist health promotion programs. Hence, the relevance of Conrad and Walsh's conclusion that

> on one level, promoting health is unassailable; few would think to oppose it. On a deeper level, though, health can be viewed as a moral discourse that reflects particular, deeply ingrained values and consequently can be used as a legitimating vocabulary for instituting changes that might otherwise be resisted.
>
> (1992: 107)

This critique can be extended by arguing that the measurement of health risks, fitness assessments and screening programs at the workplace establishes the grounds to screen out 'undesirable' employees on the basis of such factors as their body weight, lack of adherence to a self-disciplined lifestyle and recreational use of drugs. The concept of 'lifestyle,' as measured in workplace programs, therefore encompasses the private as well as the public domain (see Lupton, 1995).

Thus on the one hand health promotion, and specifically worksite health promotion may be seen as an expression of modern management ideology specifically associated with the ideas of 'empowerment' and 'self-management'; on the other hand it can be seen as a sublime way of controlling behavior in accordance with certain norms and values held by organizations and society. To this extent, a more authoritarian management regime may be easier to challenge, ignore or reject than a supporting, caring one that sets an agenda for our lifestyles (see Costea *et al.*, 2007). Health promotion comprises programs that may result in an increasingly all-encompassing network of surveillance and observation. Indeed the critical notion of empowerment in the health promotion discourse suggests individualistic meanings of rationality, autonomy and responsibility. This has paternalistic connotations by assuming that one actor, who is seen as relatively more powerful, 'empowers' a less powerful one. "The rhetoric of empowering and enabling thus serves to mask the investment and intervention of public health professionals in persuading groups to develop 'skills' and 'exercise control' over their lives" (see Lupton, 1995: 60). Accordingly health promotion can be seen as a peculiar form of management which, through the establishment of appropriate social identities forms a crucial dimension of effective social control.

However, as stressed earlier it is important not only to focus on the repressive dimensions of health promotion, but also on its productive aspect. As pointed out by Cruikshank (1999: 2), even the popular discourse on empowerment "contains the twin possibilities of domination and freedom." Empowerment has the potential to socially control people by measuring persons against a normative ideal of citizenship. Despite what was said earlier, people do have opportunities to resist. In this sense any program of empowerment can help a person to become active, not in the sense intended by these programs, but in the sense of becoming aware of potentially oppressive power structures. 'Empowered individuals' are not necessarily persons who behave in a certain manner only because an external force exerts power over them; but also because they have the power to act for themselves; they are their own masters. Certainly, technologies of health promotion operate according to a political rationality for governing people in ways that promote their autonomy, self-sufficiency and commitment. In essence, they are intended to 'help people to help themselves' to act in a morally and politically legitimate way. In this sense they are 'empowering.' If power is not external to the state of being citizen or subject, if to be self-governing is to be both citizen and subject, both subject to and the subject of government, then an 'employee' is not the antithesis of a 'manager,' capable of controlling and forming his or her destiny and life (see Friedman, 2008b).

As has already been noted, the modern 'imperative of health' is to identify dangers in order to control them (Crawford, 2004). The 'dangers' consist of humans' behaviors and attitudes that are critical to the production and re-production of social norms and values; these dangers need to be tamed and controlled and health promotion may be one mechanism through which this may be accomplished. What is interesting about health promotion is that it is directed not only at those who are sick, as is regular medical care or traditional occupational health, but all individuals. In health promotion preventive health care has moved from the medical institutions out to all major social sites and urban spaces, including schools and other educational institutions, workplaces and shopping centers. To this extent, health promotion can be regarded as a relatively comprehensive system of regulation and management. "The ideology of individual responsibility poses an alternate social control formulation. It replaces reliance on therapeutic intervention with a behavioral model which only requires good living" (Crawford, 1998: 88). In a health-valuing culture, people come to define themselves in part by how well they succeed or fail in adopting healthy practices and by the qualities of character or personality believed to support healthy behaviors. To this extent "the social state of being designated as 'healthy' are qualities that define the self," i.e. critical features of modern identity (Crawford, 2006: 402).

The knowledges and practices of health promotion that have developed in western societies, outline health promotion as a mechanism for the construction of self or self-identity and of human embodiment that would contribute to the moral regulation of organizations and societies. The famous Foucauldian relationship between power and knowledge that we discussed in the previous chapter stresses that biomedicine can be seen as a symbolic system of beliefs and a site for the reproduction of power relations. Health promotion may be conceptualized as 'governmental apparatuses,' i.e. techniques or practices of the self; specifically of learning to be a 'healthy employee.' To this extent worksite health promotion, like any social practice is creative; not merely repressive. Medical models, ideas and the medical profession have coercive elements by shaping human behaviors in certain ways, i.e. 'normalizing' it. Although this regulation may be very visible, stemming from such central authorities as occupational health services among corporations, "where this attempt at control becomes invisible is in the justification used. In the interest of health, one is largely self-policed and no force is necessary" (Lupton, 1995: 15). Failure to conform to 'healthy behavior' does not mean that one is incarcerated or fined; rather punishment consists of feelings of abnormality, guilt and anxiety.

Thus, rather than acting simply to constrain people, health promotion works to produce or 'make up' 'healthy individuals' who are capable of autonomy and 'a kind of regulated freedom.' According to this line of argument where power is a productive rather than a repressive force, 'health' has become central to the construction of subjectivities. Since people want to be 'healthy,' they tend to internalize the message of healthism without coercive intervention. This message represents a personal 'responsibilization'; here, the burden of remaining healthy is no longer on the shoulders of society (or an employer), but must be endured by individuals, who then are blameworthy if they get sick. According to this line of reasoning, it no longer makes sense to ask who are the 'victims' or who is doing the 'blaming.' Instead, everyone has become a 'victim,' where health promotion experts are not seen to be directly controlling or intervening. As observed in our study if health promotion's project is to address change at an individual or a structural level, it needs to know the 'raw material' it is working with. It needs to know what people mean by health, how they believe it affects their lives and what they feel they could or should be doing about it, in order to facilitate any effective behavior change. Health promotion experts who de facto have become managers assist in the process of understanding the self, where the healthy self is fundamentally related to power. Health promotion reconfigures the individual from being a relatively docile and passive subject, to one who is able to exercise self-control, responsibility and autonomy. Any behavioral risks that are sources of uncertainty to the reproduction of social norms and values are seen to reside in individuals, particularly their 'self control.' Indeed, Conrad and Walsh (1992: 104) suggested that health promotion "with its emphasis on disciplined lifestyle and behavior both off and on the job, encourages employees to control themselves, through internalized self-discipline and self-control."

Overall, this view on management suggests that power is a relationship that is localized, dispersed, diffused and typically disguised through the social system, operating at a micro, local and covert level through sets of specific practices. To this extent power is embodied in health promotion practices such as examinations, counselling talks and other forms of 'confession,' i.e. techniques of individualization. It is a kind of 'biopolitics,' i.e. the powers of life, of the living, and of the processes of life, where the ultimate goal is to turn the individual into an active and self-managing subject. This requires that individuals learn how to know themselves, e.g. with the guiding hand of the health promotion expert, in order to become a person who possesses the capacity for self-control, responsibility, rationality and enterprise. Rose (2001: 3) argued that contemporary biopolitics is, essentially, risk politics concerned with people's ability to contribute to societies' economic and cultural dealings, where health has become a "transactional zone between political concerns for the fitness of the nation and personal techniques for the care of the self." According to this view, health promotion programs consist of various strategies that seek to identify, treat, manage or administer those individuals or groups where risk is seen to be high. The key event in health promotion is the creation of the person 'medically at risk' that is undertaken through standard operating procedures of risk management, i.e. identification, assessment, elimination or change. What is interesting in this enterprise is that the assessment, evaluation and minimization of risk are significantly different from the obligation to care and control, or to diagnose and cure, or to befriend and reintegrate. A whole array of health promotion experts become connected up with one another in circuits of communication in order to minimize the riskiness of the individuals most intensely at risk, thus turning them into 'governable subjects' capable of bearing the burdens of liberty. The logics of risk locate the careers and identities of individuals who are the subjects of health promotion in a regime of perpetual surveillance which, however benign its intentions and objective its criteria, actually constitutes them all as actually or potentially 'risky' individuals.

In relation to this issue, one of the potentially most important ideological expressions of worksite health promotion is the discourse on 'employability' (see, e.g. Garsten and Jacobsson, 2004). It refers to individuals' capability of gaining and maintaining employment and stresses their ability to be self-sufficient actors who draw on an appropriate set of skills, experiences and attitudes. The discourse concerns a transformation of responsibility for employment from society to the individual and introduces the employable individual as a normative category with strong self-confidence and a will to act forcefully. In essence, the individual should act responsibly, independently and take initiative. The discourse is also about flexibility as the individual is constantly required to adapt his or her behavior swiftly, effectively and even happily to the constantly changing requirements that characterizes today's societies. People who for various reasons do not meet the standards of today's work organizations that can be manifested through lack of health, sickness, inadequate performance and absence constitute a growing sector of 'excluded' people (see Bauman, 1989; Beck, 2000). Not only is this group of individuals seen as lacking in certain skills and abilities; its shortages are also treated as signs of health problems. The increased significance of the health promotion discourse in contemporary working-life may fuel this development. As suggested previously the health promotion discourse's inclination to treat individuals' lifestyles and personal characteristics as key features of their health, well-being and employability implies that unhealthy lifestyles, passivity and a general lack of motivation of working on oneself to become better, more productive and able, tend to become signs of illness or disability, i.e. un-employability (cf. Crawford, 2006).

Hence, an unanticipated consequence of modern principles of worksite health promotion may be that people who are not ill from a regular biomedical point of view are still considered 'unhealthy' by not being able to live up to current social expectations and norms of employability. People who are not able to produce and re-produce social norms are in a sociological sense 'sick' (Parsons, 1951). If they cannot participate fully or according to expectations in 'constant improvements' of norms and collective behaviors, they eventually may be considered a source of 'deviance' that is to be corrected through medically-managed rehabilitation and similar mechanisms of restoration 'to desired behavior.' If this does not succeed, the individual may eventually be disposed off. In the name of health, individuals such as these may be sorted out from industry as they lack desired social skills and competencies. Worksite health promotion has not only the potential to identify desired subjectivities and identities by constructing them as 'healthy'; it has also the ability to sort out 'undesired' individuals by constructing them as 'unhealthy.' Whereas the one deals with 'healthization' the other deals with 'medicalization' (see Conrad, 1987). Both potentials are, of course, functional to any social system: the dual focus of promoting certain behaviors and of disposing off of others.

The social exclusion that may follow from health promotion is not, however, the result of any 'social execution' by a medically-conditioned management system, but of 'social suicide' (see Bauman, 1989). It is seen as self-inflicted, and the result of the individual's own choices, behaviors and attitudes. In the excluding processes, it is the excluded themselves who are the active ones. They have the responsibility for 'not having done enough,' or for just behaving incorrectly, i.e. provocatively deviating from norms and codes of healthy behavior. They must therefore be excluded to restore organized order without which no organization can function. This exclusion, created by the excluded people themselves, is not only an exercise in self-management; but also an expression of morale and ethics; indeed an act of justice. Those who decide about the formal disposing off of 'unhealthy people' at workplaces—managers in collaboration with health experts, such as company doctors and nurses can therefore feel noble and decent as they are seen as defending important values and cultural capital. In contemporary society 'unhealthy' individuals, constructed as such through modern principles of health promotion (primarily at the workplace but also in other settings), risk eventually ending up as unemployed as their unhealthy status makes them unemployable. This role effectively confirms their status as 'excluded citizens.' As already suggested, the reason for the person's unemployment is seen to reside within the individual. An unemployed person therefore needs to undergo a social transformation in order to become employable again in the sense of not only having certain technical skills, but also in the sense of being 'healthy.' Before any rehabilitation and activation can happen, however, their 'unhealthy status' must be verified, documented and enacted, otherwise their excluded status will be considered illegal and hence immoral.

It is in this context that the currently popular practice among welfare states of *medical certification of disability* fulfils its role, which is about transforming a vague group of 'unhealthy people' to a formal and comprehensible group of 'disabled people.' Indeed, medical classification of disability has become one of the major paths to aid and assistance in most welfare countries today and is targeted at people who are 'unhealthy,' thus being unable to fully fulfil social obligations such as having an employment (see, e.g. Butcher, 2002; Considine, 2001; Holmqvist, 2008). For instance, Lindsay *et al.* (2007) recently reported how the National Health Service of the UK is taking active part through health checks and similar practices to organize unemployed people under the auspices of the Public Employment Services. A key problem remains the so-called "distributive dilemma," i.e. who should benefit from society's aid and resources (see Stone, 1985)? This is 'solved' by framing unemployment as individual medical problems, i.e. by regarding unemployment as a result of a person's health, rather than the result of lack of social and economic opportunities.

By claiming that some people are disabled as an explanation for their unemployment, medicalization can be seen as an important mechanism in understanding how this individualizing enterprise in society comes about. The central practice of medical classification of disability tends to individualize unemployment, removing it from the broader social context. It can be understood with reference to the larger transformation of the welfare state into 'active societies' that emphasize people's individual responsibilities for their social situation (see e.g. Goul Andersen *et al.*, 2005; Jensen and Pfau-Effinger, 2005; Serrano Pascual, 2007), which is an ideology that is closely aligned to the practices and philosophies of health promotion, and ultimately 'self-management.'

Elm Larsen observed that

> most European welfare states have adopted some kind of activation
> policy in their overall unemployment policy. The new active line in
> labor market and social policy has been introduced under different
> names in the different European welfare states. These active measures
> have been of prime importance in reforming welfare systems and in
> stimulating or forcing labor-market participation of the unemployed
> and other social benefits claimants.

(2005: 137)

In the active society all citizens including the most 'disadvantaged ones' are
expected to be active rather than passive recipients of financial aid, hence
contributing to society's development. The activation model aims at "developing human capital and increasing the reserve workforce" as well as providing people "with moral skills, such as self-management, self-help and
self-reliance, in order to create a new kind of worker who is more flexible,
responsible and active" (Serrano Pascual, 2007: 23).

Activation policies are commonly focused on supporting disadvantaged
groups, particularly people that have been classified as 'disabled' (see, e.g.
Abberley, 2002; Overbye, 2005). The phrases 'empowerment,' 'integration,'
'rehabilitation' and 'restoration' of people with disabilities designate this
enterprise. They are all concerned with enabling unemployed disabled persons
to eventually control their own lives, hence achieving a kind of 'reformation
to normal life' (see, e.g. De Lathouwer, 2005). Disabled people, whether they
suffer from physical or mental impairments, are to be given the means
through which they by themselves can integrate in the social, economic and
cultural life of society.

In the active society, integration and empowerment is an individual
responsibility for the disabled person, but it is also a matter of concern for
society, e.g. by way of various 'welfare-to-work' programs for disabled
people, such as work training, wage allowances and sheltered employment
for disabled people (Lindert, 2004; Saunders, 2005). Government-sponsored
activities for the training, empowerment and integration of disabled people
in society are favored by the European Union, as well as by several non-
government organizations. Likewise, single governments, lobby organizations and commercial industries in many European countries favor activat-
ing labor market policies of integration of disabled jobseekers in society
(see, e.g. Abrahamson and Oorschot, 2003; Oorschot and Hvinden, 2001;
Overbye, 2005). The active society is one that ensures disabled people can
work, and enables them to do so: "'Active measures' comprise practical
efforts to assist people to find or remain in paid employment and thus
improve their prospects in the labor market" (Hvinden *et al.*, 2001: 169). It
is based on the idea that "employment is the 'royal road' to combating
exclusion and promoting inclusion" (Van Berkel *et al.*, 2002: 33). By
strengthening their skills, competencies and overall employability disabled

persons become ready and able to work when opportunities are available, hence avoiding the pitfalls of creating a permanent underclass of recipients of welfare aid that has been the experience of so many disabled men and women (see Garraty, 1978; Walters, 1997). As Dean (1995: 579) concluded: "Contemporary social policy has devised a range of institutional conditions and governmental means by which the active subject could be formed" in order to fight the specter of the self-reproduction of "a dependent group permanently living within the welfare system." Hence, since the early 1980s in many European countries there has been "a shift from *passive* to *active* measures, an emphasis on individuals' *responsibilities* to be self-sufficient vis-à-vis citizens' *rights* to social benefits, and a redefinition of policy objectives from *income maintenance* to *social inclusion*" (Gilbert, 2005: 9). An 'active line' toward the disabled person stresses how governments want to instill a new kind of responsibility where disabled people activate themselves in order to become 'normal citizens,' i.e. people fulfilling certain obligations as part of a societal contract. This is thought to be the primary means through which "unhealthy' people eventually become employable, i.e. 'healthy' again.

Appendix on Method

During the autumn of 2008 we began studying the practices and philosophies of worksite health promotion of a number of corporations and organizations: the internationally leading pharmaceutical company *Astra-Zeneca*, the Nordic telecom operator *TeliaSonera*, the government agency *Statistics Sweden*, the Nordic food and agriculture company *Lantmännen* and the state-owned retailer of wine and spirits in Sweden, *Systembolaget*. We met representatives for these organizations in Sweden whom we interviewed for around one hour each. In total, we conducted 16 semi-structured interviews. Twelve of the interviews were conducted at AstraZeneca and at this same company, we also did some 'conversational interviewing' with people of its occupational health department during lunch breaks and walks around the company's facilities, such as their recreation and sports department. At the companies we met people who worked with worksite health promotion from a more 'theoretical' point of view, primarily human resource management officers. However, the majority of interviews (11) were with corporate health experts such as company nurses, company doctors and health promotion experts. We recorded all interview data by hand and typed them into interview records, usually on the same day.

The reason as to why we chose to contact these companies was because of the fact that they had appeared in different newspaper articles on worksite health promotion in Sweden and the activities they were engaged in seemed interesting and relevant given our emerging research questions. Access was easy; no organization turned down our requests to conduct interviews. However, we could equally have ended up with other organizations, as most large employers in Sweden nowadays offer worksite health promotion programs. Our choice of cases was not entirely random, however. By contacting a number of organizations that operated in various industries (pharmaceutical, telecom, retail, agriculture and government), we hoped that we could learn some general lessons regarding what kind of worksite health promotion services were typically being offered by employers nowadays, and some typical arguments regarding their justification. Since we were not sure of exactly what we were looking for, we carried out a casual form of interviewing, where we asked respondents very broad and exploratory questions such as: (a) what kind of health promotion services do you offer? (b) why do you offer them?; (c) how are these activities organized internally?; (d) what are your expectations; (e) how are the programs related to standard human resource management activities?; and so on. As a complement to the interviews, we read documents and brochures that had been published by these organizations, both internal material for managers (e.g. instructions on how a rehabilitation process is conducted), and information to all employees of the health promotion services available. In particular, AstraZeneca and Lantmännen had extensive documentation that gave us a good view of both these organizations' commitment towards these issues as well as what concrete programs and activities were being offered. We also got the opportunity to read information on health promotion at TeliaSonera's internal website that gave us a broad picture of how that company promoted various health promotion activities internally. Of course, the degree of involvement in worksite promotion differed among these cases and the concrete approaches taken were not always comparable. For instance, one of the organizations had recently started with health promotion by offering their employees health screening sessions, another of them focused primarily on 'healthy leaders' rather than presenting a comprehensive program for all employees, and the third had worked with health promotion for many years and had institutionalized this activity into a formal department where medical experts were on the payroll.

Despite these differences, a number of preliminary common themes could, however, be deduced that were helpful to us in our efforts to specify our research questions: first, the organizations appeared to regard worksite health promotion as something different from traditional occupational health services. The traditional occupational health services were generally seen as limited to injuries and sickness incurred at work, whereas worksite health promotion "focuses on your health and lifestyle both on and off the job," as one person told us. Second, it was maintained that worksite health promotion was not primarily about the character or quality of the work environment, and the employee's interaction with it. Essentially, it was about the behaviors and attitudes of employees regarding their lifestyle and well-being. As one respondent claimed: "The focus has clearly shifted, from primarily looking at risks in the worksite to risky behavior by employees." Third, worksite health promotion programs were typically seen as "human resource management," where a traditional view of occupational health services mainly concerned with sickness, disability and rehabilitation was seen as too limited and narrow. This aspect was stressed by the fact that employees who worked on these issues in most cases formally belonged to an HRM department. One company nurse whom we met claimed that "previously we were a unit that handled concrete tasks such as work-related injuries. Nowadays we are an integrated unit in the overall personnel administration, thus we work with recruitment, promotion, dismissal and things like that."

After having completed these exploratory and tentative interviews, we thought it would be relevant to extend the study to include two corporations that sold health-promoting services such as health screening and risk management to employers in Sweden, namely the global manpower company *Adecco*, and *Previa*, the leading corporation in Sweden in occupational health services. Indeed, several of the persons interviewed at the aforementioned companies collaborated on an intense basis with these companies. We met three representatives from Adecco and four from Previa, and asked them questions regarding the market potential for selling health promotion services, the range of services offered and their character, and the way they marketed their products. These interviews lasted around one hour each and we treated the data in the same way as we had done previously. The most interesting issues for our purposes revolved around these companies' respective views on the 'ideology' of worksite health promotion, where it was stressed that worksite health promotion is a different approach to health than has been the case in the past. One manager stressed that "ideally, we do not wish to work with people who are ill or injured. We want to work with companies who are prepared to invest in furthering the health of its most important asset: its employees." Such an approach illustrates the change from a restricted focus on directly work-related health issues as observed in the companies we had studied earlier to a holistic focus on employees' lifestyles. According to this viewpoint, worksite health promotion becomes different from merely a set of medical services, thus illustrating its managerial potential. A psychologist employed by one of these companies explained: "Even though we still officially say that we investigate, counsel, and treat work-related health issues, in reality it is the combination of peoples' personalities, lifestyles, and their styles of working that our services concern." To this extent, the services appear to concern people's performance and ability to act according to certain norms and values. One of the managers said that

> of course, companies have always been searching for excellence when they hire and promote people. But today, the meaning of the word 'excellence' has much wider connotations. It is no longer just a statement about the particular set of occupational skills that a person may hold. Now, excellence is also used to characterize a person who leads a particular type of life; who is physically active, who eats proper food, who avoids unnecessary risks, who is moderate on drugs and alcohol, etc.

In sum, the interviews at Adecco and Previa confirmed much of our observations at the companies, which should, perhaps, come as no surprise given the fact that these organizations sell and promote programs of worksite health promotion.

In light of these preliminary experiences, we decided that we should make an in-depth study of worksite health promotion as an expression of management. As has already been suggested, it seemed to us that this issue had not been sufficiently explored in previous research, and that the preliminary observations made from the cases that we had been in contact with could potentially provide an interesting and relevant platform for analysis and discussion. Instead of trying to pursue a second round of interviews with the organizations mentioned previously, we contacted the Swedish company *Scania* in January 2009. During several of the interviews that we made with representatives from the other companies, Scania was mentioned as a particularly ambitious case in promoting the health of its employees. One representative told us that "if you really want to learn how worksite health promotion is conducted, you should study Scania, they know everything about it." Scania's allegedly great interest in worksite health promotion had also been stressed in the international literature on worksite health promotion (Chenoweth, 2007: 5), thus emphasizing that Scania could potentially offer some extraordinary, interesting and relevant data.

We focused on Scania's activities in the city of Södertälje (south of Stockholm), where most of its facilities including its headquarters are located. At the beginning, our approach to Scania was as tentative as it was to the other organizations, although we soon sensed that we had eventually found a case that could offer us the opportunity to deepen our analysis. The first contact was made with the manager of Scania's Health Organization (HO). We explained to him that we were interested in learning more about their health promotion activities and our interest in the interstices of management and health. He suggested that we should meet one of his employees, who was in charge of all the company's health promoting activities, as well as one health economist who was mainly concerned with statistical analysis of sick leave. This meeting was held in a similar spirit as the meetings with the other organizations, and our questions revolved around broad and exploratory issues related to Scania's health promotion. What struck us as different from the other organizations was the relative importance attached to worksite health promotion by Scania as witnessed by the number of people employed by the HO unit. Several of the other companies also worked intensely on worksite health promotion but their efforts were limited to specified projects that were conducted in collaboration with external health promotion services providers such as Adecco and Previa. Scania, on the other hand, had all resources 'in house' and seemed to regard health promotion as an integral and daily part of its operations.

As a consequence of these early experiences, we suggested to the manager of the HO unit at Scania that we would undertake a study of Scania's health promotion "regarded as a strategic issue," as we chose to label it. After some clarification of our ideas and perspectives, he agreed to the project and in February 2009 we embarked on a pilot study that would eventually serve as the platform for a more comprehensive study. The pilot study consisted of 23 semi-structured interviews with corporate health experts working at the HO unit: company doctors, nurses, ergonomic experts, work environment engineers, health promotion experts and behavioral specialists. We also met the manager of the HO unit and his management team that consisted of three more persons, as well as administrative staff. Interviews with each individual lasted for around one hour and they focused on discussing such concrete aspects as, what kind of programs are offered; what are the expectations of these programs; how are activities organized; how is the HO organized and managed; what are the goals and strategies of that unit, etc. As done previously, we recorded all data by hand and typed them into interview records. In addition to these formal interviews, we met personnel of the HO unit during a number of lunch breaks and during coffee, where we could discuss issues of relevance more informally. We also had a number of telephone and e-mail conversations with some of the health professionals, usually after we had interviewed them personally.

We participated in seven meetings held by this unit's so-called health teams. A health team consists of representatives from different 'health disciplines,' e.g. nurses, doctors, physiotherapists and behavioral experts. Participation in these meetings complemented the interviews by giving us the opportunity to listen to what issues were regularly attended to, what problems and challenges they experienced internally and in the external communication and collaboration with the rest of Scania, what projects and ideas they were focusing on, etc. In addition, we got access to Scania's internal website that consisted of a host of documents related to the programs and activities of the HO, e.g. what courses (e.g. in "healthy eating") were available, what services such as health screening were offered, and so on. We also collected a number of other documents, e.g. Scania's personnel magazine that offered stories on the activities of the HO unit, as well as brochures issued by the HO unit that described to the rest of Scania the activities of this particular unit. Overall, the pilot study gave us a broad and basic picture of the purpose and vision of the HO unit, what activities were central, what professions were involved and their role in the larger organization of Scania.

After having conducted this study, we reported in a meeting to the management team of the HO unit that, in very short and simplified terms, we thought that an overarching interpretation of this unit's activities was that of a 'cultural engineering department' that certainly was concerned with traditional occupational health services in terms of preventing diseases and rehabilitating sick and disabled employees, but that primarily could be understood as a mechanism for promoting a certain ideal of 'employeeship' and identity at Scania. Their response to this preliminary conclusion was enthusiastic. In order for us to more closely analyze that hypothesis, we suggested that we should continue studying the activities of the HO unit by doing interviews and meeting people throughout Scania, thus not only focusing on the activities of the HO unit and its programs and activities. The manager of the HO unit agreed to this and offered us a number of names of production managers in various facilities whom we could contact in order to get started; but we soon got a 'free hand' to talk to anyone in the organization that could help us shed light on our emerging questions. We decided that we should meet employees and managers who had experiences of interaction with the health experts of the HO both in the production facilities, i.e., the factories, and at offices by talking to people at Scania's sales department, research and development, and information technology unit.

We did interviews with the following categories of people: seven human resource management officers, i.e., people working at Scania's various human resources units that were all located at the various facilities; 18 shopfloor supervisors and line managers; 31 employees; and 16 persons in various functions (such as members of Scania's so-called Scania Production System's Office, one member of the executive team, a number of people working at Scania's department for training and education, etc.). Most of the interviews lasted around one hour, with the exception of employees and supervisors and line managers whom we met either on the shopfloor, or during visits to Scania's sports and recreation facility (named 'Gröndal'). These interviews were more informal and 'conversational' in the sense that they took place when people carried out their work, or during breaks, etc. Our ambition with this phase of the study was to get a better view of what concrete activities and practices the HO unit was involved in; how this unit was considered; how it interacted in concrete projects and activities with the rest of Scania; and what were the expectations of it. We asked, for instance, questions on how and why managers contacted the HO unit and what they thought about their daily interaction with them, and what was the relation of employees to the HO unit and how were their experiences with the health professionals. We complemented the interviews by participating in a number of activities (approx. 20 hours) as offered by the HO unit, such as Scania's Health School, courses in nutrition and physical exercise at Gröndal, courses in mental training and 'balance in life,' etc. During these sessions we got the opportunity to experience how Scania's health experts concretely inter-acted with the personnel, e.g. by listening to how they presented the content of the courses, what questions were being asked by the participants, how participants experienced the courses, how they participated, etc.

When the formal study was completed in the summer of 2009, we pre-sented our tentative interpretations and conclusions to the management team of the HO unit. Later on, we gave the manager of the unit the oppor-tunity to read and comment on the empirical chapters (Chapters 4–7) of a draft version of this book, and he clarified some minor factual issues on the unit's activities and its formal organization.

Of course, there is a large literature that gives very helpful advice on doing qualitative case study research, for instance on how to design archival studies, how to do interviews, how to set up and analyze questionnaires, and how to pursue various types of observations (see, e.g. Barley, 1990; Eisenhardt, 1989; Miles and Huberman, 1994; Yin, 1994). When completing this study we benefited from this literature in a casual sense. As our research design very much evolved as the study progressed, we did not strictly adhere to any a priori rules of how to complete the data collection and analysis. However, we have tried to be faithful to the following idea: "Careful observation of ordinary organizational life is critical. If there are insights to be found in modern perspectives on organizational choice, they are borrowed from the fine detail of good field observations" (March, 1981: 207). Overall, we would say that our study is "based on the view that one can only understand the social world by obtaining first-hand knowledge of the subject under investigation ... by 'getting inside' situations and involving oneself in the everyday flow of life" (Burrell and Morgan, 1979: 6). Other qualitative studies have been very helpful in informing us on how to concretely exercise various methods. In Scandinavia, there is a long tradition of doing field studies among students of organization; thus we have been lucky to work in an environment where much valuable experience is at hand. Likewise, we have found much guidance and inspiration in a number of informative case studies on related topics (e.g. Kunda, 1992; Orr, 1996).

If we were to 'label' our research process by using the terminology that is popular in the literature on qualitative methods, perhaps we have followed what Strauss and Corbin (1990) and Miles and Huberman (1994) have respectively labelled 'an iterative process,' i.e., a travel back and forth between the data and an emerging structure of theoretical arguments and ideas. As we have pursued our research, we have concurrently worked with 'empirical data' and 'theory.' We started off with some conceptual ideas on 'modern management' that made worksite health promotion a potentially interesting case; these ideas proved to some extent useful when trying to make sense of this phenomenon. But we also continuously experienced surprise and puzzlement when pursuing our study, thus stressing a need for further conceptual analysis by reading relevant literature.

Bibliography

Abberley, P. (2002), "Work, Disability, Disabled People and European Social Theory." In C. Barnes, M. Oliver and L. Barton (Eds), *Disability Studies Today*, Cambridge: Polity, 120–38.

Abrahamson, P. and W. Oorschot (2003), "The Dutch and Danish Miracles Revisited: A Critical Discussion of Activation Policies in Two Small Welfare States," *Social Policy and Administration*, 37, 288–304.

Adler, P. (2001), "Market, Hierarchy, and Trust: The Knowledge Economy and the Future of Capitalism," *Organization Science*, 12, 2, 215–34.

Aglietta, M. (1979), *A Theory of Capitalist Regulation. The US Experience*, London: Verso.

Albrecht, G. L. (2002), "American Pragmatism, Sociology and the Development of Disability Studies." In C. Barnes, M. Oliver and L. Barton (Ed.), *Disability Studies Today*, Cambridge: Polity, 18–37.

Alvesson, M. and H. Willmott (2002), 'Identity Regulation as Organizational Control: Producing the Appropriate Individual,' *Journal of Management Studies*, 39, 5, 619–44.

Antonovsky, A. (1987), *Unraveling the Mystery of Health : How People Manage Stress and Stay Well*, San Francisco, CA: Jossey-Bass.

Argyris, C. and D. A. Schön (1996), *Organizational Learning II*, Reading, MA: Addison-Wesley Publishing Company.

Arnold, J. and L. J. Breen (2006), "Images of Health." In S. Sheinfeld Gorin and J. Arnold (Eds), *Health Promotion in Practice*, San Francisco, CA: Jossey-Bass, 3–20.

Baker, W. (1992), "The Network Organization in Theory and Practice." In N. Nohiria, and R. Eccles (Eds) *Networks and Organizations, Structure, Form and Action*, Boston, MA: Harvard Business School Press.

Ballard, K. and M. A. Elston (2005), "Medicalization: A Multi-Dimensional Concept," *Social Theory and Health*, 3, 228–41.

Bandura, A. (1997), *Self-efficacy: The Exercise of Control*, Basingstoke: Freeman.

Barker, J. (1993), "Tightening the Iron Cage: Concertive Control in Self-Managing Teams," *Administrative Science Quarterly*, 38, 408–37.

Barley, S. R. (1990), "Images of Imaging: Notes on Doing Longitudinal Field Work," *Organization Science*, 3, 220–47.

Barley, S. R. and G. Kunda (1992), "Design and Devotion: Surges of Rational and Normative Ideologies of Control in Managerial Discourse," *Administrative Science Quarterly*, 37, 363–99.

Barratt, E. (2002), "Foucault, Foucauldianism and Human Resource Management," *Personnel Review*, 31, 2, 189–204.

——(2003), "Foucault, HRM and the Ethos of the Critical Management Scholar," *Journal of Management Studies*, 40, 5, 1069–87.

Barcelona Declaration on Developing Good Workplace Health Practice in Europe, http://www.enwhp.org/publications.html (Last accessed April 19, 2010).

Bartlett, C. and S. Ghoshal (1997), *The Individualized Corporation*, New York: Harper Business.

Bauman, Z. (1989), *Modernity and the Holocaust*, Cambridge: Polity.

Beck, U. (2000), *The Brave New World of Work*, Cambridge: Polity.

Bell, D. (1973), *The Coming of Post Industrial Society, A Venture in Social Forecasting*, New York: The Perseus Books Group.

Benveniste, G. (1994), *Twenty-first Century Organization: Analyzing Current Trends, Imaging the Future*, San Francisco, CA: Jossey-Bass.

Bernstein, S. D. (2003), "Positive Organizational Scholarship: Meet the Movement," *Journal of Management Inquiry*, 12, 266–71.

Blaxter, M. (1990), *Health and Lifestyles*, London: Routledge.

Braverman, H. (1974), *Labour and Monopoly Capital. The Degradation of Work in the 20th Century*, New York: Monthly Review.

Brousseau, K. R., M. J. Driver, K. Eneroth and R. Larsson (1996), "Career Pandemonium: Realigning Organizations and Individuals," *Academy of Management Executive*, 10, 52–66.

Bull, M. (1990), "Secularization and Medicalization," *British Journal of Sociology*, 41, 245–61.

Bunton, R. (1992), "More than a Woolly Jumper: Health Promotion as Social Regulation," *Critical Public Health*, 3, 4–11.

Bunton, R. and G. Macdonald (1992), "Introduction." In R. Bunton and G. Macdonald (Eds), *Health Promotion. Disciplines, Diversity and Developments*, London: Routledge, 1–8.

Burawoy, M. (1979), *Manufacturing Consent*, Chicago, IL: University of Chicago Press.

Burrell, G. and G. Morgan (1979) *Sociological Paradigms and Organisational Analysis: Elements Of The Sociology Of Corporate Life*, Aldershot: Ashgate.

Burrell, G. and G. Morgan (2000), "Two Dimensions: Four Paradigms." In P. Frost, A. Y. Lewin and R. L. Daft (Eds), *Talking About Organization Science*, London: Sage, 107–22.

Butcher, T. (2002), *Delivering Welfare*, second edition, Buckingham: Open University Press.

Cameron, K. S. and A. Caza (2004), "Contributions to the Discipline of Positive Organizational Scholarship," *American Behavioral Scientist*, 47, 731–39.

Carlson, S. (1951), *Executive Behavior,* Stockholm: Stockholm School of Economics.

Carlson, S. and P. Ernmark (1951), "A Swedish Case Study on Personnel Relations," Stockholm: Stockholm School of Economics.

Casey, C. (1999), "'Come Join our Family': Discipline and Integration in Corporate Organizational Culture,' *Human Relations*, 52, 2, 155–78.

Caza, B. B. and A. Caza (2008), "Positive Organizational Scholarship. A Critical Theory Perspective," *Journal of Management Inquiry*, 17, 21–33.

Center for Positive Organizational Scholarship at the University of Michigan, http://www.bus.umich.edu/Positive/ (Last accessed April 19, 2010).

Chenoweth, D. H. (2007), *Worksite Health Promotion*, New Bern, NC: Human Kinetics.

Concise Oxford Dictionary (1999), Edited by Judy Pearsall, tenth edition, Oxford: Oxford University Press.

Conrad, P. (1987), "Wellness in the Work Place: Potentials and Pitfalls of Work-site Health Promotion," *The Milibank Quarterly*, 65, 255–75.

——(1994), "Wellness as Virtue: Morality and the Pursuit of Health," *Culture, Medicine and Psychiatry*, 18, 385–401.

——(2007), *The Medicalization of Society*, Baltimore, MD: The Johns Hopkins University Press.

Conrad, P. and D. C. Walsh (1992), "The New Corporate Health Ethic: Lifestyle and the Social Control of Work," *International Journal of Health Services*, 22, 1, 89–111.

Considine, M. (2001), *Enterprising States. The Public Management of Welfare-to-Work*, Cambridge: Cambridge University Press.

Corker, M. and T. Shakespeare(2002), *Disability/postmodernity: Embodying Disability Theory*, London: Continuum.

Costea, B., N. Crump and K. Amiridis (2007), "Managerialism and 'Infinite Human Resourcefulness': a Commentary on the 'Therapeutic Habitus,' 'Derecognition of Finitude' and the Modern Sense of Self," *Journal For Cultural Research*, 11, 5, 245–64.

Covaleski, M., M. Dirsmith, J. Heian and S. Samuel (1998), "The Calculated and the Avowed: Techniques of Discipline and Struggles over Identity in Big Six Public Accounting Firms," *Academy of Science Quarterly*, 43, 293–327.

Crawford, R. (1980), "Healthism and the Medicalization of Everyday Life," *International Journal of Health Services*, 10, 3, 365–88.

——(1998), "You are Dangerous to Your Health: The Ideology and Politics of Victim Blaming." In L. Mackay, K. Soothill and K. Melia (Eds), *Classic Texts in Health Care*, 84–89.

——(2000), "The Ritual of Health Promotion." In S. J. Williams, J. Gabe and M. Calnan, *Health, Medicine and Society*, 219–35.

——(2004), "Risk Ritual and the Management of Control and Anxiety in a Medical Culture," *Health: An Interdisciplinary Journal for the Social Study of Health, Illness and Medicine*, 8, 505–28.

——(2006), "Health as a Meaningful Social Practice," *Health: An Interdisciplinary Journal for the Social Study of Health, Illness and Medicine*, 10, 4, 401–20.

Cruikshank, B. (1999), *The Will to Empower*, Ithaca: Cornell University Press.

Davidow, W. and M. Malone (1992), *The Virtual Corporation*, New York: Harper Collins.

Davies, C. (1989), "Goffman's Concept of the Total Institution: Criticisms and Revisions," *Human Studies*, 12, 77–95.

Davies, J. and G. Macdonald (1998), "Beyond Uncertainty: Leading Health Promotion into the Twenty-First Century." In J. Davies and G. Macdonald (Eds), *Quality, Evidence and Effectiveness in Health Promotion: Striving for Certainties*, London: Routledge.

De Lathouwer, L. (2005). "Reforming the Passive Welfare State: Belgium's New Income Arrangements to Make Work Pay in International Perspective." In P. Saunders (Ed.), *Welfare to Work in Practice. Social Security and Participation in Economic and Social Life*, Aldershot: Ashgate, 129–54.

Dean, M. (1995), "Governing the Unemployed Self in an Active Society," *Economy and Society*, 24, 4, 559–83.

Deetz, S. (1998), "Discursive Formations, Strategized Subordination and Self-surveillance." In A. McKinley and K. Starkey (Eds), *Foucault, Management and Organization Theory*, London: Sage.

Diamante, T., S. M. Natale and M. London (2006), "Organizational Wellness." In S. Sheinfeld Gorin and J. Arnold (Eds), *Health Promotion in Practice*, San Francisco, CA: Jossey-Bass, 460–93.

Docherty, P., J. Forslin and R. Shani (Eds) (2002), *Creating Sustainable Work Systems: Emerging Perspectives and Practice*, London: Routledge.

Downie, R. S., C. Tannahill and A. Tannahill (1996), Health Promotion. Models and Values, second edition, Oxford: Oxford University Press.

Drucker, P. (1988), "The Coming of the New Organization," *Harvard Business Review*, 66, (January–February), 45–53.

Du Gay, P. (2000), *In Praise of Bureaucracy*, London: Sage.

Du Gay, P., G. Salaman, and B. Rees (1996), "The Conduct of Management and the Management of Conduct: Contemporary Managerial Discourse and the Constitution of the 'Competent' Manager," *Journal of Management Studies*, 33, 3, 263–82.

Edwards, R. (1979), *Contested Terrains: The Transformation of the Workplace in the 20th Century*, New York: Basic Books.

Eisenhardt, K. M. (1989), "Building Theories from Case Study Research," *Academy of Management Review*, 14, 4, 532–50.

Elm Larsen, J. (2005), "The Active Society and Activation Policy: Ideologies, Contexts and Effects." In J. Goul Andersen, A. M Guillemard, P. H. Jensen and B. Pfau-Effinger (Eds), *The Changing Face of Welfare. Consequences and Outcomes from a Citizen Perspective*, Bristol: The Policy Press, 135–50.

European Network for Workplace Health Promotion, www.enwhp.org (Last accessed April 19, 2010).

Foucault, M. (1980), Power/Knowledge: Selected Interviews and Other Writings 1972–77, London: Harvester Wheatsheaf.

——(1997), Ethics, Subjectivity and Truth, Essential Works of Michel Foucault Vol. 1, New York: New Press.

Friedman, S. D. (2006), "Learning to Lead in All Domains of Life," *American Behavioral Scientist*, 49, 9, 1270–97.

——(2008a), *Total Leadership: Be a Better Leader, Have a Richer Life*, Boston: Harvard Business Press.

——(2008b), "Be a Better Leader, Have a Richer Life," *Harvard Business Review*, April, 112–18.

Garraty, J. A. (1978), *Unemployment in History*, New York: Harper & Row.

Garsten, C. and C. Grey (1997), "How to Become Oneself: Discourses of Subjectivity in Post-bureaucratic Organizations," *Organization*, 4, 2, 211–28.

Garsten, C. and K. Jacobsson (2004), "Learning to be Employable: An Introduction." In C. Garsten and K. Jacobsson (Eds), *Learning to be Employable. New Agendas on Work, Responsibility and Learning in a Globalizing World*, Houndmills: Palgrave, 1–22.

Giertz, E. (1991), Människor i Scania under 100 år : industri, arbetsliv och samhälle i förändring, Stockholm: Norstedts.

Gilbert, N. (2005), "Protection to Activation: The Apotheosis of Work." In P. Saunders (Ed.), *Welfare to Work in Practice. Social Security and Participation in Economic and Social Life*, Aldershot: Ashgate, 9–22.

Gillies, P. (1998), "Effectiveness of Alliances and Partnerships for Health Promotion," *Health Promotion International*, 13, 99–120.

Goldmann, R. B. (1976), *A Work Experiment: Six Americans in a Swedish Plant*, New York: Ford Foundation.

Goul Andersen, J., A. M Guillemard, P. H. Jensen and B. Pfau-Effinger. (2005), (Eds), *The Changing Face of Welfare. Consequences and Outcomes from a Citizen Perspective*, Bristol: The Policy Press.

Green, L. W. and M. W. Kreuter (1999), *Health Promotion and Planning: An Educational and Ecological Approach*, third edition, Mountain View, CA: Mayfield Publishing.

Green, L. W., B. D. Poland and I. Rootman (2000), "The Settings Approach to Health Promotion." In B. D. Poland, L. W. Green and I. Rootman (Eds), Settings for Health Promotion, London: Sage, 1–43.

Grey, C. and C. Garsten (2001), "Trust, Control and Post-bureaucracy," *Organization Studies*, 22, 2, 229–50.

Halal, W. (1994), "From Hierarchy to Enterprise: International Markets are the New Foundation of Management," *Academy of Management Executive*, 8, 69–83.

Hanson, A. (2007), *Workplace Health Promotion: A Salutogenic Approach*, Bloomington, IN: Authorhouse.

Harvey, D. (1982), *The Limits to Capital*, New York: University of Chicago Press.

——(1989), *The Condition of Post-Modernity*, Oxford: Blackwell Publishing.

Heckscher, C. (1994), "Defining the Post-Bureaucratic Type." In C. Heckscher and A. Donnellon (Eds), *The Post-Bureaucratic Organization*, Thousand Oaks, CA: Sage.

——(1995), *White Collar Blues: Management Loyalties in an Age of Corporate Restructuring*, New York: Basic Books.

Heckscher, C. and A. Donnellon (1994) (Eds), *The Post-bureaucratic Organization. New Perspectives on Organisational Change*, London: Sage.

Hodgson, D. E. (2004), "Project Work: The Legacy of Bureaucratic Control in the Post-Bureaucratic Organization," *Organization*, 11, 1, 81–100.

Hogget, P. (1991), "A New Management in the Public Sector?," *Policy and Politics*, 19, 243–56.

Holmqvist, M. (2008), *The Institutionalization of Social Welfare. A Study of Medicalizing Management*, New York: Routledge.

——(2009), "Corporate Social Responsibility as Corporate Social Control. The Case of Work-site Health Promotion," *Scandinavian Journal of Management*, 25, 68–72.

Holmqvist, M. and C. Maravelias (2006) (Eds), *Hälsans styrning av arbetet*, Lund: Studentlitteratur.

Höpfl, H. M. (2006), "Post-bureaucracy and Weber's 'Modern' Bureaucrat," *Journal of Organizational Change Management*, 19, 8–21.

Hvinden, B., M. Heikkilä and I. Kankare (2001), "Towards Activation? The Changing Relationsip between Social Protection and Employment in Western Europe." In M. Kautto, J. Fritzell, B. Hvinden, J. Kvist and H. Uusitalo (Eds), *Nordic Welfare States in the European Context*, London: Routledge, 168–97.

Jensen, P. H. and B. Pfau-Effinger (2005), "'Active' Citizenship: The New Face of Welfare." In J. Goul Andersen, A. M. Guillemard, P. H. Jensen and B. Pfau-Effinger (Eds), *The Changing Face of Welfare. Consequences and Outcomes from a Citizen Perspective*, Bristol: The Policy Press, 1–14.

Kallinikos, J. (2003), "Work, Human Agency and Organizational Forms: An Anatomy of Fragmentation," *Organization Studies*, 24, 4, 595–618.

Kanter, R. (1990), *When Giants Learn to Dance*, London: Unwin Hyman.

Kira, M. (2000), *From Intensive to Sustainable Work Systems—a Literature Review*, Department of Industrial Economics and Management, Stockholm: Royal Institute of Technology.

Koelen, M. A. and A. W. van den Ban (2004), *Health Education and Health Promotion*, Wageningen: Wageningen Academic Publishers.

Korp, P. (2002), *Hälsopromotion: En stude av hälsofrämjandets institutionalisering*, Göteborg: BAS.

——(2008), "The Symbolic Power of 'Healthy Lifestyles'," *Health Sociology Review*, 17, 18–26.

Kunda, G. (1992), *Engineering Culture: Control and Commitment in a High-Tech Corporation*, Philadelphia, PA: Temple University Press.

Lalonde, M. (1974), "A New Perspective on the Health of Canadians." Downloaded from www.hc-sc.gc.ca on September 9, 2009.

Levinthal, D. A. and J. G. March(1993), "The Myopia of Learning," *Strategic Management Journal*, 14, (Special Issue: Organizations, Decision Making and Strategy) (Winter), 95–112.

Lindert, P. H. (2004), *Growing Public*, Cambridge: Cambridge University Press.

Lindsay, C., R. W. McQuaid, and M. Dutton (2007), "New Approaches to Employability in the UK: Combining 'Human Capital Development' and 'Work First Strategies'?," *Social Policy*, 36, 539–60.Lisbon Statement on Workplace Health in Small and Medium-Sized Enterprises, http://www.enwhp.org/publications.html (Last accessed April 19, 2010).

Lupton, D. (1995), *The Imperative of Health. Public Health and the Regulated Body*, London: Sage.

——(1997), "Foucault and the Medicalization Critique." In A. Peterson and R. Bunton (Eds), *Foucault and Medicine*, London: Routledge, 95–110.

Luthans, F. (2002), "Positive Organizational Behavior: Developing and Managing Psychological Strengths," *Academy of Management Executive*, 16, 57–72.

Luxembourg Declaration on Workplace Health Promotion in the European Union (2007), Downloaded from www.enwhp.org on October 15, 2009.

MacDonald, T. H. (1998), Rethinking Health Promotion, A Global Approach, London: Routledge.

MacIntosh, R., D. MacLean and H. Burns (2007), "Health in Organization: Towards a Process-Based View." *Journal of Management Studies*, 44, 206–21.

Maravelias, C. (2003), "Post-Bureaucracy—Control through Professional Freedom," *Journal of Organizational Change Management*, 16, 5, 547–66.

——(2009), "Health Promotion and Flexibility: Extending and Obscuring Power in Organizations," *British Journal of Management*, 20, 1, 194–203.

March, J. G. (1981), "Decision Making Perspective." In A. H. Van de Ven and W. F. Joyce (Eds), *Perspectives on Organization Design and Behavior*, New York: John Wiley and Sons, 205–48.

March, J. G. and H. A. Simon (1993), *Organizations*, New York: Blackwell Business.

Mayo, E. (1933), *The Human Problems of an Industrial Civilization*, New York: Basic Books.

Merton, R. K. (1940), "Bureaucratic Structure and Personality," *Social Forces*, 18, 560–68.

Miles, M. B. and A. M. Huberman (1994), *Qualitative Data Analysis*, second edition, London: Sage.

Mills, C. Wright (1951), *White Collar: The American Middle Class*, New York: Oxford University Press.

Mintzberg, H. (1998), "Covert Leadership: Notes on Managing Professionals," *Harvard Business Review*, 76, 140–47.

Mises, L. von (1944), *Bureaucracy*, New Rochelle: Arlington.

Nettleton, S. and R. Bunton (1995), "Sociological Critiques of Health Promotion." In R. Bunton, S. Nettleton and R. Burrows (Eds), The Sociology of Health Promotion. Critical Analyses of Consumption, Lifestyle and Risk, London: Routledge, 41–58.

Norstedt, J-P and S. Agurén (1973), *Scania-rapporten*, Stockholm: SAF.

New Foundation of Management, *Academy of Management Executive*, 8, 69–83.

O'Donnell, M. P. (2002), "Preface." In M. P. O'Donnell (Ed.), *Health Promotion in the Workplace*, New York: Delmar, xiv–xxvi.

O'Leary, A. (1985), "Self-efficay and health," *Behavior Research and Therapy*, 23, 437–51.

Ollier-Malaterre, A. (2009), Book Review. *Human Resource Management*, 48, 4, 665–67.

Oorschot, W. and B. Hvinden (2001), *Disability Policies in European Countries*, The Hague: Kluwer Law International.

Orr, J. (1996), *Talking About Machines : An Ethnography of a Modern Job*, Ithaca: ILR Press.

Overbye, E. (2005), "Dilemmas in Disability Activation and How Scandinavians Try to Live With Them." In P. Saunders (Ed.), *Welfare to Work in Practice. Social Security and Participation in Economic and Social Life*, Aldershot: Ashgate, 155–72.

Parish, R. (1995), "Health Promotion. Rhetoric and Reality," In R. Bunton, S. Nettleton and R. Burrows (Eds), *The Sociology of Health Promotion. Critical Analyses of Consumption, Lifestyle and Risk*, London: Routledge, 13–23.

Parsons, T. (1951), *The Social System*, New York: The Free Press.

Perlow, L. A. (1998), "Boundary Control: The Social Ordering of Work and Family in a High-tech Corporation," *Administrative Science Quarterly*, 43, 328–57.

Perry, N. (1974), "The Two Cultures and the Total Institution," *The British Journal of Sociology*, 25, 345–55.

Peters, T. (1992), *Liberation Management*, Basingstoke: Macmillan.

Peterson, C. and A. J. Stunkard (1989), "Personal Control and Health Promotion," *Social Science Medicine*, 28, 819–28.

Polanyi, M. F. D., J. W. Frank, H. S. Shannon, T. J. Sullivan and J. N. Lavis (2000), "Promoting the Determinants of Good Health in the Workplace." In B. D. Poland, L. W. Green and I. Rootman (Eds), *Settings for Health Promotion*, London: Sage, 138–74.

Procter, S. (2005), "Organizations and Organized Systems. From Direct Control to Flexibility." In S. Ackroyd, R. Batt, P. Thompson and P. S. Tolbert (Eds), *The Oxford Handbook of Work and Organization*, Oxford: Oxford University Press, 462–84.

Quick, J. C., M. Macik-Frey and C. L. Cooper (2007), "Managerial Dimensions of Organizational Health: The Healthy Leader at Work," *Journal of Management Studies*, 44, 189–205.

Raeburn, J. and I. Rootman (1998), *People-Centred Health Promotion*, Chichester: Wiley.

Roberts, L. M. (2006), "Shifting the Lens on Organizational Life: The Added Value of Positive Scholarship," *Academy of Management Review*, 31, 292–305.

Roberts, L. M., G. Spreitzer, J. Dutton, R. Quinn, E. Heaphy and B. Barker (2005), "How to Play your Strengths," *Harvard Business Review*, January, 1–7.

Rose, N. (1999), *Governing the Soul*, second edition, London: Free Association Books.

——(2001), "The Politics of Life Itself," *Theory, Culture and Society*, 18, 6, 1–30.

Saunders, P. (2005), "Welfare to Work in Practice: Introduction and Overview." In P. Saunders (Ed.), *Welfare to Work in Practice. Social Security and Participation in Economic and Social Life*, Aldershot: Ashgate, 1–8.

Savage, C. (1996), *Fifth Generation Management, Co-creating through Virtual Enterprising, Dynamic Teaming, and Knowledge Networking*, Boston, MA: Butterworth and Heinemann.

Scania, www.scania.com (Last accessed April 19, 2010).

Seedhouse, D. (1997), *Health Promotion. Philosophy, Prejudice and Practice*, New York: Wiley.

——(2004), *Health Promotion: Philosophy, Prejudice and Practice*, New York: John Wiley.

Serrano Pascual, A. (2007), "Reshaping Welfare States: Activation Regimes in Europe." In A. Serrano Pascual and L. Magnusson (Eds), *Reshaping Welfare States and Activation Regimes in Europe*, Brussels: Peter Lang, 11–34.

Sewell, G. and B. Wilkinson (1992), "'Someone to Watch Over Me': Surveillance, Discipline and the Just-in-Time Labour Process," *Sociology*, 26, 2, 271–89.

Shenkar, O. (1996), "The Firm as a Total Institution: Reflections on the Chinese State Enterprise," *Organization Studies*, 17, 885–907.

Simon, H. A. (1997), *Administrative Behavior*, fourth edition, New York: The Free Press.Skrabanek, P. (1994), *The Death of Humane Medicine and the Rise of Coercive Healthism*,The Social Affairs Unit,Suffolk: Crowley.

Sloan, R. P., J. C. Gruman and J. P. Allegrante (1987), *Investing in Employee Health. A Guide to Effective Health Promotion in the Workplace*, San Francisco, CA: Jossey-Bass.

Smith, A. (1994), *Wealth of Nations*, Oxford: Oxford University Press.

Smith, V. (1997), "New Forms of Work Organization," *Annual Review of Sociology*, 23, 315–39.

Sonnenstuhl, W. J. (1986), *Inside and Emotional Health Program*, Ithaca: ILR Press.

Spreitzer, G., K. Sutcliffe, J. Dutton, S. Sonensheim and A. M. Grant (2005), "A Socially Embedded Model of Thriving at Work," *Organization Science*, 16, 537–49.

Stark, L. R. (1994), "The Shelter as 'Total Institution'," *American Behavioral Scientist*, 37, 553–62.

Stone, D. A. (1985), *The Disabled State*, Basingstoke: MacMillan.

Strauss, A. and J. Corbin (1990), *Basics of Qualitative Research: Techniques and Procedures for Developing Grounded Theory*, second edition, London: Sage.

Strecher, V. J., B. McEvoy DeVellis, M. H. Becker and I. M Rosenstock (1986), "The Role of Self-efficacy in Achieving Health Behavior Change," *Health Education Behavior*, 13, 74–92.

Taylor, F. W. (1998), *The Principles of Scientific Management*, New York: Dover.

The New York Times (2008), "Hot Ticket in B-School: Bringing Life Values to Corporate Ethics." May, 29. Downloaded from www.nytimes.com on October 10, 2009.

Thomas, C. (2002), "Disability Theory: Key Ideas, Issues and Thinkers." In C. Barnes, M. Oliver and L. Barton (Ed.), *Disability Studies Today*, Cambridge: Polity, 38–57.

Thorogood, M. and Y. Coombes (2004), "Introduction." In M. Thorogood and Y. Coombes, *Evaluating Health Promotion: Practice and Methods*, second edition, Oxford: Oxford University Press, 3–9.

Thorogood, N. (1992), "What is the relevance of sociology for health promotion?." In R. Bunton and G. Macdonald (Eds), *Health Promotion. Disciplines, Diversity and Developments*, London: Routledge, 54–79.

Tones, K. and J. Green (2004), *Health Promotion. Planning and Strategies*, London: Sage.

Total Leadership, www.totalleadership.org (Last accessed April 19, 2010).

Townley, B. (1994), *Reframing Human Resource Management: Power, Ethics and the Subject at Work*, London: Sage.

Tracy, S. J. (2000), "Becoming a Character for Commerce. Emotion Labor, Self-Subordination, and Discursive Construction of Identity in a Total Institution," *Management Communication Quarterly*, 14, 90–128.

Van Berkel, R., I. Hornemann Moller, and C. C. Williams. (2002). "The Concept of Inclusion/Exclusion and the Concept of Work." In R. Van Berkel and I. Hornemann Moller (Eds), *Active Social Policies in the EU. Inclusion through Participation?* Bristol: The Policy Press, 15–44.

Volberda, H. (1998), *Building the Flexible Firm*, New York: Oxford University Press.

Walters, W. (1997), "The 'Active Society': New Designs for Social Policy," *Policy and Politics*, 25, 221–34.

Walton, R. E. (1985), "From Control to Commitment in the Workplace," *Harvard Business Review*, March/April, 77–84.

Weare, K. (1992), "The contribution of education to health promotion." In R. Bunton and G. Macdonald (Eds), *Health Promotion. Disciplines, Diversity and Developments*, London: Routledge, 102–25.

Weber, M. (1978), *Economy and Society*, Vols. 1 and 2, Los Angeles, CA: California University Press.

Weick, K. E. (1969), *The Social Psychology of Organizing*, Reading, MA: Addison-Wesley.

WHO (1986), The Ottawa Charter for Health Promotion. Downloaded from www.who.int on January 27, 2010.

——(2010), "Health Promotion." Downloaded from www.who.int on January 27, 2010.

WHO Regional Office for Europe (2005), http://www.euro.who.int/publications (Last accessed April 19, 2010).Whyte, W. H. (1956), *The Organization Man*, Philadelphia, PA: Penn.

Wilkinson, C. (1999), "Management, the Workplace and Health Promotion: Fantasy or Reality?," *Health Education Journal*, 58, 56–65.

Willmott, H. (1993), "Ignorance is Strength; Slavery is Freedom: Managing Culture in Modern Organizations," *Journal of Management Studies*, 30, 5, 512–55.

Yin, R. K. (1994), *Case Study Research*, second edition, London: Sage.

Ziglio, E., S. Hagard and J. Griffiths (1999), "Health Promotion Development in Europe: Achievements and Challenges," *Health Promotion International*, 15, 143–54.

Zola, I. K. (1972), "Medicine as an Institution of Social Control." *Sociological Review*, 20, 487–504.

Zoller, H. M. (2003), "Working Out. Managerialism in Workplace Health Promotion," *Management Communication Quarterly*, 17, 2, 171–205.

Index